Al Ward's Photoshop Productivity Toolkit:

Over 600 Time-Saving Actions

Al Ward's Photoshop®
Productivity Toolkit:
Over 600 Time-Saving Actions

Al Ward

SYBEX®   San Francisco • London

Associate Publisher: DAN BRODNITZ
Acquisitions Editor: BONNIE BILLS
Developmental Editor: PETE GAUGHAN
Production Editor: LESLIE E.H. LIGHT
Technical Editor: RICHARD LYNCH
Copyeditor: PAT COLEMAN
Compositor: MAUREEN FORYS, HAPPENSTANCE TYPE-O-RAMA
Graphic Illustrator: RAPPID RABBIT
CD Coordinator: DAN MUMMERT
CD Technician: KEVIN LY
Proofreaders: NANCY RIDDIOUGH, LAURIE O'CONNELL
Indexer: LYNNZEE ELZE
Cover design: JOHN NEDWIDEK, EMDESIGN
Cover photographs: 2nd from right: AL WARD; Far right: CMCD LIBRARY;
   All others: JOHN NEDWIDEK, EMDESIGN

Software License Agreement: Terms and Conditions

*To my loving wife Tonia, to Ali, and to Noah;
it is a joy and privilege to share my life with you.*

 # Acknowledgments

Thanks to all the great people at Sybex: Bonnie Bills, who believed not only in the idea behind the book but in the author's ability to write it. Also to Pete, Leslie, Dan, and Rodney; I appreciate your dedication and support throughout the process. Special thanks to Sen, who has become one of my favorite people on the planet! To Rodnay and everyone else, thanks again, and I look forward to working with you all in the future.

Special thanks to the contributors to the CD contents of the book and to Richard Lynch for his care and dedication on the technical edits. These contributions and Richard's dedication really help to fill out the project, and I couldn't have done this without you. Thanks again!

Thanks go to my buddies in the business: Colin Smith, Richard Lynch, Robert Anselmi, Scott Kelby, Jeff Kelby, Dave Cross, Stacy Behan and everyone at NAPP, and others too numerous to mention.

To the members and visitors to my website, ActionFx.com: you have kept me driven to continue pursuing this course, and for that I'm grateful to every one of you. Updates are coming soon!

To my family and friends, extended and scattered though they may be, you know who you are!

Special thanks to my fellow compatriots at the MLMBC.

Finally (but certainly not least on the list) to my God and my Savior the Lord Jesus Christ, who allows this simple Montana boy to not only do what he loves, but make a living at it as well. Psalm 40:11.

Contents

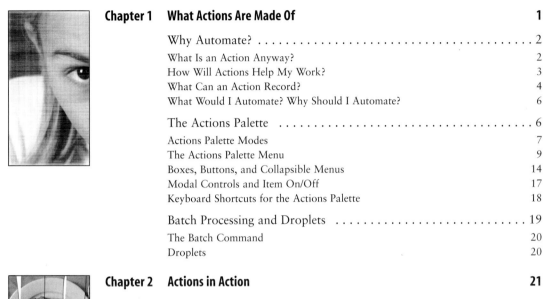

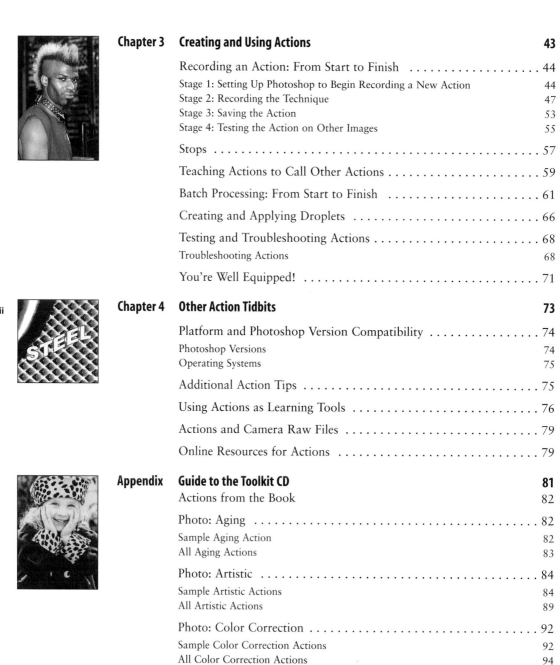

"Actions can help you bypass  the learning curve."

Introduction

When I first began working with Photoshop, actions were the lure to get me excited about the program. In a sense you could say I owe my career to Adobe, to Photoshop, and to actions in particular.

How can actions change a person's life? Well, it was because of my website dedicated to actions that I was introduced to Scott Kelby. Scott is one in a million: in exchange for some work on the NAPP website (http://photoshopuser.com), he allowed me to write for *Photoshop User* magazine, and thus my life forever changed.

Actions started this course, so it is my humble pleasure to write on the subject. Actions are far more powerful than they have been given credit for, and this book will show you how you can streamline your work with these seemingly simple macros.

Who Should Use This Book

In short, everybody who uses Photoshop. Not that I'm pitching for sales (although sales are a good thing). The primary reason people of all stripes and level of expertise with the software should read this is that actions can improve the way all levels of users interact with the software.

New users can use actions to learn about Photoshop, much the way they taught me when I first started working with the software. Actions can help intermediate to advanced users streamline production by automating time-consuming processes and techniques they have already learned and simply need to apply quickly. Actions save time, and for people producing graphics, time is money. Actions can help you both learn the program and techniques and bypass the learning curve altogether.

Making the Most of the Toolkit: What's Inside

The printed content of *Al Ward's Photoshop Productivity Toolkit* consists of four chapters, a guide to the companion CD, and a special color section.

Chapter 1: What Actions Are Made Of In this chapter, you'll learn what actions are, why they are important, and why you should use them. We will take a look at the Actions palette and discover what can be recorded and what cannot, and I'll discuss each item/command available to you that deals with actions and what they all mean.

Chapter 2: Actions in Action Find out how to load, save, play, and edit actions. You will learn about palette modes and even how to edit commands within actions and apply new settings to your recorded techniques and processes.

Chapter 3: Creating and Using Actions This chapter teaches you how to record and construct your own actions—even actions that call other actions!—and how to apply them to multiple files for maximum time-saving results. You will create an action as I walk you through the process from start to finish. You will also learn how to add, remove, and alter commands, as well as use helpful features such as Stops to their full effect. Batch processing, Droplets, and troubleshooting are also covered in this chapter.

Chapter 4: Other Action Tidbits You need to know how actions interoperate—or don't—across different versions of Photoshop and different operating systems. This chapter also presents information on converting actions to text files for use as learning tools and finishes with some valuable online resources specific to action fans.

Guide to the Toolkit CD This part of the book contains examples of some actions found on the CD, as well as a folder-by-folder breakdown of the CD's contents. Included are source image files and actions mentioned in the chapters. Several folders contain additional resources such as layer styles, shapes, and brushes, and several contributors have supplied actions for your use as well. In all, there are more than 1000 cool plug-ins for Photoshop, as well as an interesting piece of software, called Action Dex, included for Windows users that will help organize and categorize your actions. Very cool!

Color Section The 32-page color section showcases color-oriented material from the CD actions. This section focuses on some of the very cool things the actions from the CD can do for you: to duplicate an effect seen here, simply load it into Photoshop, click Play, and voilà!

The Toolkit CD

The CD that accompanies this book features more than 600 actions that I created, as well as additional actions and software from third parties. Also included are stock images found in the book (supplied by PhotoSpin.com at http://photospin.com) and other Photoshop add-ons such as layer styles, brushes, and custom shapes to use in your work or modify to suit your particular needs.

How to Reach the Author

I appreciate your comments and would like to hear from you. You can reach me through the publisher at www.sybex.com or via my website at http://actionfx.com. Now get out there and start automating!

About the Author

Al Ward, a certified Photoshop Addict and Webmaster of Action FX Photoshop Resources (http://actionfx.com), hails from Missoula, Montana. A former submariner in the U.S. Navy, Al now spends his time writing about graphics and creating add-on software for Adobe Photoshop and Photoshop Elements.

Al is the author of *Photoshop for Right Brainers: The Art of Photo Manipulation* (Sybex, 2004) and of *Adobe Photoshop Elements 2 Special Effects*. He is coauthor of *Photoshop Most Wanted*, *Photoshop Most Wanted 2*, and *Foundation Photoshop 6.0*. He has also contributed to half a dozen more Photoshop books.

Al is a featured columnist in *Web Designer* magazine and contributes to *Practical Web Projects* magazine. He has written for *Photoshop User* magazine and for many Photoshop-related websites, including the National Association of Photoshop Professionals (NAPP) official site (http://photoshopuser.com); Planet Photoshop (http://planetphotoshop.com); graphics.com (http://graphics.com); and PhotoshopCafe (http://photoshopcafe.com).

Al was a panelist at the Photoshop World 2001 Los Angeles Conference and contributes to the official NAPP website as the Actions area coordinator.

Al lists Scott Kelby, Editor-In-Chief of *Photoshop User*, as his hero; coffee as his favorite food group; and sleep as the one pastime he'd like to take up some day. In his off time, he enjoys his church, his family, fishing the great northwestern United States, and scouring the Web for Photoshop-related topics.

What Actions Are Made Of

1

Doesn't it always seem as if there are more tasks to perform during the day than the hours will allow? I find myself in this situation regularly. Such is the life I've chosen; if I'm not in front of my computer, the bills don't get paid. If there were a way to automate day-to-day tasks, I could focus on the important work or be off enjoying my family. Fortunately, Adobe created actions, which allow busy Photoshop and ImageReady users to record the steps of a task for replay later. Complete a task successfully once, and the software can duplicate those steps on another image or group of images. Now that's what I call living!

Chapter Contents

Why Automate?

Why should you automate? The primary reason comes down to the old axiom from *Poor Richard's Almanac* (written by Benjamin Franklin, for those keeping score): time is money. Say you have 1500 photos that need a simple levels adjustment or batch resizing to thumbnails. Tackling such a task could take days, regardless of how simple the process: the sheer volume of photos needing processing requires hours upon hours of valuable time. A Photoshop action, on the other hand, can take care of the process in hours, and you need not be present during the work.

I will be covering the Actions palette in depth later in this chapter. Let me say this up front: actions are far more useful than they have been given credit for. I've been a champion of these little scripts for years, and in these pages I'll demonstrate why actions are not only cool to play with, but are powerhouses of production that will save both time and money for the actions-savvy photographer.

What Is an Action Anyway?

I recently looked up the word *action* in the dictionary, and, as is usually the case with English words, *action* renders at least eight separate definitions. Nearly all the definitions imply an act or movement that leads to or ends in a desired result. That being the case, the word *action* is appropriate when applied to Photoshop's ability to record steps taken within the software.

An action is, in its simplest form, a small file created by Photoshop (with input from the user) to which the software assigns a particular extension. This extension (.atn) simply tells Photoshop that the file is an action that the software can read and repeat. Programmers familiar with macros will grasp the similarity right away. When you load a prerecorded action into the Actions palette and play it, every command in that action is carried out in the same sequence in which it was originally recorded.

An action works just like a recording. When you create an action, every Photoshop function you perform is added to the "tape" until you stop the recording process, and it can then be played back and repeated without the need for the user to go through every step again. The icons on the bottom of the Actions palette when in List mode reflect the recording idea, as shown in Figure 1.1.

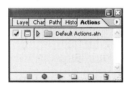

Figure 1.1 The Actions palette in List mode, showing the Stop, Record, and Play buttons

Above all else, actions are time- and money-savers that, when recorded and implemented properly, help you increase production and give you more time to pursue other avenues or aspects of your work. They may seem intimidating to those unfamiliar with them, but actions are easy once you get a handle on them. When you begin to see the power of these little recordings, I'm sure you will wonder how you ever lived without them.

How Will Actions Help My Work?

Actions can help in a number of ways. It doesn't matter if you are a photographer who wants the best resolution for your portraits or a web designer looking for continuity in your website graphics; actions will increase your productivity. Remember, time is money.

Actions can be customized to fit particular workloads. For instance, a print house could hire a Photoshop guru to create an entire set of Photoshop actions specific to the needs of their business. These actions will allow the print house to batch process groups of images to meet the preprint requirements for specific magazines and periodicals. As the requirements change and develop, the actions can be edited accordingly. Even actions not originally developed to the printer's specifications (for example, third-party actions found online or elsewhere) can be edited, customized, and resaved with the new settings.

Actions are also useful because they can be shared with others. Say you have a friend who has developed a process in Photoshop that turns every photo it is applied to into a Picasso. If that friend records the technique as an action, he can then give it to you. You load it into the Actions palette on your computer, and, barring any system or software compatibility issues, you can duplicate the effect on your own photos with a click of a button. (See Chapter 4 for information on compatibility.)

I find one other thing about actions incredibly useful. An action is, in effect, a text file. With the .atn extension, it cannot be viewed by a text editor; however, Adobe has incorporated a way in which to convert an action or a group of actions to a text format. As a result, you can make a hard copy of the entire process: every setting, every command, every filter used to make a certain effect or adjustment can be saved as a text file, opened in text-editing software such as Notepad, and then printed as a hard-copy tutorial for you to use at your leisure. Keep in mind that, in order to use the actions in Photoshop, you must save them as normal .atn files: the text files serve as informational documents only and cannot be loaded back into the program once saved as text. Granted, you may not need this feature for actions you create yourself, except as a reminder of how you organized the commands. But when it comes to actions you've gathered from other sources, this is a powerful feature, because it allows you to view all the commands and settings used. This is an excellent learning tool that will be covered in Chapter 4. Once you have the process down, you can save any action on the CD included with this book as a text file and print it for your training library. Talk about double the bang for your buck!

What Can an Action Record?

Actions are extremely versatile in that they allow you to record almost everything—I repeat, *almost*. Not all settings, commands, and tools can be recorded, but you can work around these limitations. Actions are so versatile, in fact, that you can record steps into actions in many ways. You can use the menus, or, if you are savvy with keyboard shortcuts, you can record with these.

 Note: Photoshop does not recognize some keyboard shortcuts on an operating system other than the one on which the action is recorded. If you intend for your actions to play on both Windows and Macintosh, using the File menus is the way to go.

Table 1.1 is a neat list of which tools can and cannot be recorded with actions.

▶ **Table 1.1** Action-able Status of Photoshop Tools

Can Be Recorded	Can't Be Recorded
Audio Annotation	Blur, Sharpen, Smudge
Color Sampler	Clone Stamp, Pattern Stamp
Crop	Dodge, Burn
Eyedropper	Eraser, Background Eraser
Gradient	Healing, Patch, Color Replacement
Lasso	History Brush, Art History Brush
Magic Eraser	Paintbrush
Magic Wand	Path Selection, Direct Selection
Marquee	Pen
Move	Pencil
Note	Zoom
Paint Bucket	
Polygon	
Shape	
Slice	
Type	

Basically, any tool that requires you to paint, manually select, erase, or alter the image/layer with the mouse cannot be recorded; you must still perform most of these functions manually.

That said, in one situation you can apply paint with the action. If, for instance, you create a path or a path from a selection, you can stroke the path with a Paintbrush so that the paint is applied along the path. As mentioned, there is usually a workaround for things that "can't" be done with actions: you may need to use a little intuition to find it. An action is only as intelligent or complex as the creator makes it: the firmer your grasp on how the software works, the more functionality you can squeeze from actions.

Modal Tools and Operations

Some tools and commands in Photoshop are *modal* in nature. That is, they use units specified for the ruler to judge where in an image an operation should take place or tool function be applied. Modal tools and operations typically require you to press Enter (Windows) or Return (Mac) to accept the change or setting; transformations using the Transform commands are good examples of this.

If your action will be run on images of different size or dimension, change the ruler units to percent before recording the action. When you do so, the modal-specific commands in the action play back in the same general area in each image.

You can record most operations and filters in actions, as well as settings and commands from within palettes. For instance, while recording an action, you can select another action to be played; I'll cover this topic in Chapter 3.

For those commands that cannot be recorded (painting and toning, option settings for tools, view and window commands), you can use the Insert Menu Item command. In effect, this stops the action and lets you perform the nonrecordable function. Spell-check is a good example of this; user input is required in this instance, and Photoshop won't know which version of *there, their,* or *they're* you want. Again, this will be covered in depth later.

One other item will help you when developing actions: a Stop. A Stop lets you insert messages into the action so that while the action is replaying, you can tell the user to perform certain functions that are otherwise nonrecordable, tell them to change or apply text, or simply give them information about the action. You can even advertise your website, leave your e-mail, or give out any other information you would like. Another excellent use for a Stop is a personal note to help you remember what you were doing at a certain point.

What Would I Automate? Why Should I Automate?

Since Photoshop allows you to automate nearly every function in the software, this is a difficult question to answer. Repetitive tasks that you perform frequently without adjustment to settings are clear candidates for actions. Resizing, image quality techniques, preparing items for display online or in print, creating text styles for watermarks, cropping, rotating, and applying filters are all good contenders.

Ultimately, the question of what you should or should not automate is up to you. You know better than I which commands you use frequently and at what setting. Some people record actions for the simplest functions; some create them for techniques that are extremely advanced and time-consuming.

For instance, let's take a quick look at keyboard shortcut combinations. Keyboard shortcuts let you select and apply/reapply tools or settings and are intended to be easy, correct? The problem is that there are so many keyboard shortcuts it is difficult to remember a fraction of them! You recall the ones you use frequently, but those you use less frequently are long forgotten or hard to track down.

Case in point: let's say you want to rerun the Transform command with duplicate data from the original layer. The Windows shortcut keys are Ctrl+Shift+Alt+T; on a Mac, they are Command+Shift+Option+T. It is almost more difficult to use the shortcut than it is to simply run the desired process from the Edit menu. In some cases, the shortcut combinations are so complex my fingers have a hard time reaching all the keys.

In Photoshop CS, you can now change and customize your keyboard shortcuts, and this is great, provided no other commands are already assigned to that shortcut. With so many keyboard combinations already assigned, this is difficult to say the least. With an action, however, you can record the setting and assign a new shortcut key combination. You can then either click Play and run the action or press the new key combination. You can assign a shortcut to an action that simply attaches it to a function key (F1, F2, and so on) or combines a function key with Shift, Command/Ctrl, or both, allowing for 60 keyboard shortcuts that can be assigned to actions.

What should you automate and why? Anything that will save you time in the long run, whether tool shortcuts or extended image-processing techniques. After a while you will know what works best for your situation and what will benefit your work most. Actions are for your benefit; use them to your advantage.

The Actions Palette

You control and manage Photoshop actions using the Actions palette (see Figure 1.2). You use this palette to play, record, edit, and delete individual actions, as well as load saved action sets.

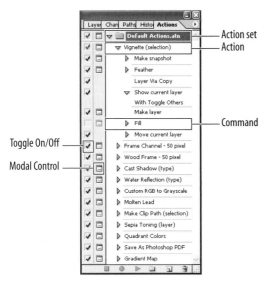

Action set —
Action —
Command —
Toggle On/Off —
Modal Control —

Figure 1.2 The Actions palette

Note: Photoshop actions can be saved only in action sets. A set can contain one or more actions. ImageReady does not allow you to group actions together in sets; Photoshop gives you this option so that your actions can be better organized.

You can access the Actions palette in two ways: choose Window > Actions, or use the Windows shortcut key combination Alt+F9. If the palette is visible but not active (docked with other palettes or resident in the Palette Well), simply click the Actions tab to bring it to the foreground.

After an overview of palette modes and the Actions palette menu, this chapter will move into the body of the Actions palette itself, breaking down and describing each item in the palette while in List mode.

Actions Palette Modes

The Actions palette has two modes or states: Button and List. This chapter primarily focuses on List mode, as you can do a lot more when the palette is in that state. Before getting into List mode, Button mode warrants a glance.

Button mode displays all the actions loaded into the palette as color-coded buttons; the colors are assigned by the action's creator. In Button mode, you cannot edit the action; you are given the option of running the action only by clicking the button. Figure 1.3 shows the Actions palette in Button mode, with Adobe's default actions loaded.

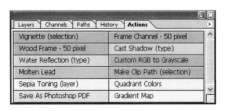

Figure 1.3 The Actions palette Button mode with Photoshop's default actions

In Button mode, you can add prerecorded actions to the palette using the Actions palette menu. This is discussed in more detail shortly.

I mentioned color coding the actions. When creating an action, you can assign three items to it, which are then visible when the palette is in Button mode: color coding, shortcut key assignment, and, of course, the action's name. Figure 1.4 again shows the Actions palette in Button mode with the default actions loaded. The difference here is that I've assigned a shortcut key combination to the Vignette action at the top of the palette. In Windows, you can now run the action by pressing Ctrl+F2.

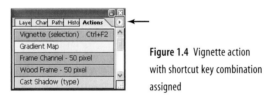

Figure 1.4 Vignette action with shortcut key combination assigned

There is really not much else to say about Button mode; your options are fairly limited when using the palette in this mode. Button mode is there for your benefit, however; finding and playing actions in List mode can be frustrating, as all commands are listed. When many actions are loaded into the palette and their lists expanded, tracking down the action you want to play can become confusing. Button mode displays the action as a button only; just click and watch Photoshop go to work.

You use the Actions palette menu to change the Actions palette from Button to List mode and vice versa. To access the Actions palette menu, click the small button in the upper-right corner of the Actions palette (see the arrow in Figure 1.4).

With the menu open, you can change between Button and List modes by selecting Button Mode from the list. To change the mode, simply select Button Mode again. When checked, Button mode is on; when unchecked, the palette switches to List mode (see Figure 1.5).

Figure 1.5 Change the palette mode by selecting and deselecting Button mode from the Actions palette menu

Button mode is there for your convenience; later, you will learn (while creating actions) how to color code your buttons for organization as well as assign shortcut keys.

The Actions Palette Menu

When you get into actually creating actions, the Actions palette menu is going to be your best friend. It is here that you have the most control over the actions and action sets you create.

The palette menu (see Figure 1.6) is sectioned into groups of commands. I'll break them down into small manageable bites; if you are already familiar with the operation of actions, this discussion will be a good refresher.

Figure 1.6 The Actions palette menu

The top section of the menu has two commands that deal with the palette's location and mode:

Dock To Palette Well Selecting this command relocates the palette and groups it with the palettes resident in the Palette Well in the upper-right corner of Photoshop, on the far right side of the Options bar (see Figure 1.7). The Palette Well lets you "dock" palettes to this area to help clean the work area of palettes that can clog things up fairly quickly and make it difficult to navigate the image you are working on. To access the Actions palette, click the appropriate tab, bringing that palette to the fore of the group. Clicking the small arrow to the right of the palette's name will again open the Actions palette menu.

Button Mode As mentioned earlier, you can change between Button and List modes by selecting Button Mode from the palette menu.

Figure 1.7 The Palette Well helps clear your desktop of palettes that may obscure your work area.

The next two groups, or divisions, of action commands in the Actions menu are those that allow you to create, delete, record, or otherwise edit an action:

New Action Opens the New Action dialog box (see Figure 1.8). Here you can specify attributes for a new action (its name, the existing set in which the action will be placed, the function key assignment, and the color). A new action must be placed in a set. Click Record or Cancel to close this dialog box. When you click Record, everything you do in Photoshop beyond that point is recorded into the action until you stop recording.

Figure 1.8 The New Action dialog box. Here you can name the action, designate which set it is to be placed in, assign function or shortcut key combinations for quick playback, and assign color coding for organization that can be viewed when the Actions palette is in Button mode.

New Set Opens the New Set dialog box (see Figure 1.9) and creates a new action set, in which actions can be placed. Actions can only be saved in sets. The only option available in this dialog box is the naming of the set.

Figure 1.9 The New Set dialog box

Duplicate Creates a duplicate action set or a duplicate action, depending on which is highlighted in the Actions palette. The duplicate takes up residence in the Actions palette.

Delete Deletes the active action or set.

Play Plays the selected action. If a set is selected rather than an action, this command becomes unavailable.

Start Recording Begins recording the steps of the action. This command becomes available only when an action is selected in the Actions palette. This command is unavailable if a set is selected in the palette. Once you click Start Recording, everything you do in Photoshop beyond that point is recorded in the action until you cease recording.

Record Again Allows you to rerecord an action and set new values for the commands in the action. The original action will play, but the dialog boxes contained therein will open, allowing you to change or accept the settings in each.

Insert Menu Item Inserts commands accessed by menus. Some commands, such as tool options, window commands, and view commands cannot be recorded in an action. If for some reason these need to be accessed in the course of playing an action, you can use this command to insert commands accessed by menus. The Insert Menu Item command does not execute until the action is played, and no values for the command are recorded. For commands with dialog boxes, these will appear during playback, and the action will pause, allowing for user input. When you click OK, the action proceeds. Hitting Cancel stops the action at that step and you must manually restart.

Insert Stop Inserts messages directly into actions, one of the single most useful tools available to action creators. The types of messages and subjects are entirely up to you. You can insert Stops during recording or place them in the action later. Figure 1.10 shows an example of a Stop message inserted in the Record Stop dialog box. The Allow Continue check box gives the user the option of simply continuing the action beyond the Stop. When this check box is not checked, the action will cease running until some function is performed and the action started manually again. Stops that are placed at the end of an action will have no need to continue, so this may be unchecked (see Figure 1.11).

Figure 1.10 The Record Stop dialog box with an introductory message. Notice that the Allow Continue check box is checked.

Figure 1.11 A closing Stop message example. The action does not proceed beyond this point, so the Allow Continue check box is unchecked.

Insert Path Inserts a path in the document the action is working on. You can create or import the path and then select Insert Path. If you create the path, you must use this command in order for the action to recognize it. This is particularly helpful in Photoshop CS when your action calls for you to type in a path, a function that was not available in earlier versions of the software.

The next section allows you to select options for the active action and playback options for the Actions palette.

Action Options Opens the Action Options dialog box (see Figure 1.12), which is nearly identical to the New Action dialog box. In this dialog box, you can change the name of the selected action, assign a function key combination, and assign a color to the action's button. The only differences between this and the New Action dialog box are the ability to choose which set the action is placed in (the action will still reside in its current parent set) and the OK button, which replaces the Record button. When you click OK, the change to the action is made without recording further.

Figure 1.12 The Action Options dialog box, which is similar to the New Action dialog box, with a couple of differences

Playback Options Opens the Playback Options dialog box (see Figure 1.13) in which you can specify how the action will perform on playback. For instance, select Accelerated, and when the action is played, it quickly applies the action commands to the image without showing each step in the workspace. When you select Step By Step, you can see each command applied to your image in the workspace, though the speed at which this happens depends on the commands applied. (Render filters, some blurs, and so forth take longer to apply, so the action can slow down at these points.) Selecting Pause For allows you to insert the amount of time, in seconds, between the application of each command in an action. This is helpful in tracking errors in an action, but I only recommend you use this option while troubleshooting. Pausing playback for even one second can slow the action intolerably.

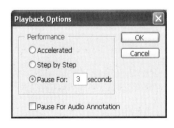

Figure 1.13 The Playback Options dialog box. Select the Pause For option only for troubleshooting.

Pause For Audio Annotation Pauses the action and plays back the annotation. You can insert audio annotations in actions if an audio annotation exists. Deselect this option to bypass audio annotation playback.

The next section in the Actions palette menu deals with the Actions palette itself, with the exception of Save Actions. These are self-explanatory:

Clear All Actions Removes all action sets and their actions from the Actions palette.

Reset Actions Restores Adobe's default actions to the palette. Options are offered for removing any other action sets that may be loaded or adding the default actions to the palette, leaving the loaded action sets in place. If other action sets are loaded, a dialog box will appear asking if you want to proceed with this command. You can click Accept (replaces the loaded actions with the defaults), Cancel (retains the Actions palette in its current state), or Append (adds the default actions to those currently loaded). See Figure 1.14.

Figure 1.14 The Reset Actions dialog box allows you to restore the default actions or add the default actions to those currently residing in the Actions palette.

Load Actions Opens the Load dialog box and allows you to locate and load actions saved on your hard drive or on a CD into the Actions palette. Actions in the palette will not be replaced; the selected action set will be amended to those currently residing in the Actions palette. Figure 1.15 shows a Load dialog box in Windows directed to the Adobe Photoshop CS actions. These actions can be found in this folder:

`\Program Files\Adobe\Photoshop CS\Presets\Photoshop Actions`

Replace Actions Replaces the action sets currently loaded in the Actions palette with those you select from another source, such as third-party actions saved to your hard drive or on a CD.

Save Actions Allows you to save your actions after recording or editing is complete.

Note: The action set in which the action resides must be selected in the Actions palette in order for the Save Actions option to be available. Again, actions can only be saved in sets.

The final area of the palette menu, found at the bottom, shows those action sets that are saved to the `Photoshop Actions` folder in the `Presets` subfolder. Selecting one of these (by default they are Commands, Frames, Image Effects, Production, Text Effects, and Textures) amends that set to those already resident in the Actions palette.

Figure 1.15 Selecting the Load Actions command lets you search your hard drive for additional actions and add them to the Actions palette for playback.

You can add to this list by saving action sets to the Photoshop Actions folder in the Presets subfolder. Once you save the action set, you need to reboot Photoshop in order for the action set to appear in this listing. Once the program is restarted, the action set (not the individual actions in the set) appear in the list (see Figure 1.16).

Figure 1.16 Adding action sets to the \Presets\ Photoshop Actions folder will, after restarting the program, allow those sets to appear at the bottom of the Actions palette menu for quick loading to the Actions palette.

That, in the proverbial nutshell, is what the Actions palette menu consists of. As you go through later chapters, you will be working with this menu extensively and begin creating actions that are functional, cool, and transferable across platforms for others to use and enjoy.

Boxes, Buttons, and Collapsible Menus

List mode is the primary mode for action creators. Here you operate modal controls, handle recording, and change or delete commands. An action is only as smart as you create it to be, and understanding the controls within the Actions palette will help you make some smart actions indeed.

A first glance at the Actions palette in List mode can be scary to those unfamiliar with it. All those boxes, buttons, commands, and so forth—what can they all mean? Let me break things down for you by looking at each item in the palette and then the components for those items.

At the top of the Actions palette hierarchy is an action set. In Figure 1.17, you can see three sets loaded into the palette: Default Actions.atn, Al's Killer Metal Text, and Image Size Enhancer. Action sets work like folders; they store actions. Each set can contain one or more actions.

Figure 1.17 The Actions palette in List mode, showing three action sets loaded

Clicking the small arrow next to Default Actions.atn expands the set so that you can see and select the actions in the set—sort of like opening a folder to glance at the contents (see Figure 1.18).

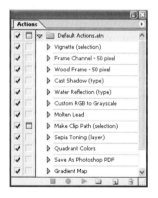

Figure 1.18 The Actions palette in List mode, with an action set expanded to view the actions in the set

Keep in mind that, if the set is selected, you will not be able to play the actions. Some get frustrated because they don't understand the distinction between a set and an actual action and are stymied when they select a set and do not have the option to play. Remember, a set is just like a folder; you must select an action in order for the play or record controls to be available.

You can also expand, or open, the actions themselves to view the commands within the action in the order they were recorded. Again, clicking the small arrow to the left of the action name opens the action for viewing (see Figure 1.19).

Figure 1.19 An action expanded to display the commands that will be applied to the image when the action is played

Last, you can open each command in like manner to view the settings for that command. Figure 1.20 shows an open action set with an expanded action, and the commands in that action are expanded to display their settings. The Feather command lists the amount of feather applied to the selection, the Fill command lists the color, opacity, and mode, and so on.

Figure 1.20 Commands within an action expanded to display the settings of each command in the action

You can also expand or collapse all actions in a set or all commands in an action at once. To do so, use the shortcut key combinations. For Windows, Alt+click the arrow corresponding to the action or set you want to view; on a Mac, Option+click.

Note: To recap, click the triangle to the left of the set, action, or command to expand or collapse that item in the Actions palette.

You can also select and play more than one action at a time. To select multiple contiguous actions, Ctrl+click (Windows) or Command+click (Mac) a group of actions in the palette. To select multiple discontiguous actions (see Figure 1.21), Shift+click each action you want to run.

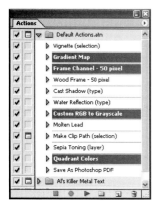

Figure 1.21 You can select multiple contiguous or discontiguous actions and play them in the order they appear in the Actions palette.

Note: If you plan on selecting and then running more than one action for playback, you want to ensure that those actions are in the correct order in the Actions palette. Photoshop will play the topmost selected action first, move to the next selected action down the list, and so on. If the actions are out of order, you most likely will not get the results you expect. If you find one or more actions in the wrong position for sequential playback, simply highlight the action with the mouse in the palette and drag it into place.

Modal Controls and Item On/Off

Modal controls, indicated in the Actions palette as filled or empty boxes immediately to the left of the action or set, affect only those commands that involve dialog boxes. A filled modal control indicator tells Photoshop to pause at that point and display the dialog box for that command so that the user can input new settings if need be. When a modal control is unfilled, the action proceeds without showing the dialog box, using instead the original settings applied during recording.

Figure 1.22 shows the Vignette action expanded with modal controls for the Feather and Make Layer commands turned on and the Make Snapshot, Fill, and Move Current Layer modal controls turned off.

Figure 1.22 An action with some modal controls turned on and others off

You can also turn on all the modal controls in an action set by clicking the modal control indicator to the right of the set's name. When this indicator is red, some or all of the modal controls in the set are off; clicking this indicator turns the modal control gray and activates every modal control in the set. You can do the same with individual actions (turn all controls on or off), or you can simply select those you would like turned on inside the action.

The Toggle Item On/Off check box is self-explanatory: If the check box next to an action set, action, or command in an action is checked, that item is available. If unchecked, it is bypassed, just like a light switch. Figure 1.23 shows the Actions palette with some items unchecked/turned off.

Figure 1.23 The Actions palette with some action commands toggled off and some toggled on

You can use shortcut key combinations to turn all modal controls on or off and toggle all items on/off: Alt/Option+click the set or action modal control or Toggle Item On/Off check box.

Of course, if you toggle an action off, it will not be available for playback. Also, if a command is toggled off, the action will bypass that command completely. That is something to keep in mind when troubleshooting, but I'll cover that later in the book.

Keyboard Shortcuts for the Actions Palette

Nearly everything in Photoshop has a shortcut assigned to it, and Photoshop CS gives you the ability to generate combinations of your own. Several shortcuts directly affect the Actions palette. Table 1.2 explains those shortcuts.

▶ **Table 1.2** Keyboard Shortcuts for the Actions Palette

Result	Windows	Mac OS
Toggles all but the selected command off, or toggles all commands on.	Alt+click the check mark next to a command.	Option+click the check mark next to a command.
Toggles selected modal controls on and toggles all other modal controls either on or off depending on their state.	Alt+click.	Option+click.

Result	Windows	Mac OS
Displays the Set or Action Options dialog box.	Double-click set or actions. Alt+double-click set or action in ImageReady.	Double-click set or actions. Alt+double-click set or action in ImageReady
Play the entire action.	Ctrl+double-click an action.	Command+double-click an action.
Collapse/expand all components of an action so that the commands and settings can be viewed in the palette.	Alt+click the triangle.	Option+click the triangle.
Play a single command in an action.	Ctrl+click the Play button.	Command+click the Play button.
Create a new action and begin recording without confirmation. (This simply prevents the dialog box from appearing, creating a new action with Record turned on.)	Alt+click the New Action button.	Option+click the New Action button.
Select contiguous items of the same kind. (Select two or more action sets, two or more actions, two or more commands, etc.)	Shift+click the action/command.	Shift+click the action/command.
Select noncontiguous items of the same kind. (Select two or more action sets, two or more actions, two or more commands, etc.)	Ctrl+click the action/command.	Command+click the action/command.

If you want to set up your own shortcuts, choose Edit > Keyboard Shortcuts and assign your own combinations manually. Bear in mind that Photoshop already uses hundreds of shortcuts, so it may be difficult to find combinations that are not in use.

Batch Processing and Droplets

Using actions to process multiple images for a specific result will be covered in depth in Chapter 3, but it is important to understand the relationship between actions, the Batch command, and droplets. Actions can be run independent of the Batch command or droplets, but the Batch command and droplets require actions.

These three elements work together to give you control over the editing or correction of multiple images, refining your workload and saving incredible amounts of time if used together correctly. The Batch command and droplets, although similar, are two separate entities; they are placed together here for readability.

I have covered actions, at least on an introductory level, so let me briefly explain batch processing and droplets.

The Batch Command

The Batch command lets you play an action on a folder of images or on groups of folders. You can also use the Batch command to import and process images from other sources, such as scanners and digital cameras with action-compatible plug-in modules, and you can import PDF images from capture software programs such as Adobe Acrobat Capture.

The power of Photoshop actions, for a photographer, actually resides in the Batch command. Batch processing lets you correct multiple images while taking care of other tasks, leaving Photoshop to process and save the selected files without user input. You can even leave Photoshop to do the work while you're at home sleeping; when you return to work the next day, you can rest assured, if everything performed properly, that all 1500 images have been corrected, resized, and saved to a new folder with the originals intact, for one example. Chapter 3 covers batch processing in depth.

Droplets

Droplets are similar in operation to the Batch command, but are distinguished from the former in that droplets are actually small applications. A droplet has its own icon that can be saved to a folder or to the desktop. You can then drag an image file or a folder of images to the icon, and Photoshop will open (if it isn't already) and process each image in the folder. Although a droplet is an application, it cannot process images independently of Photoshop. Droplets will be covered in depth in Chapter 3.

Actions in Action

You would think that the best way to learn actions is simply to read on the subject and then begin creating them. In my experience, this was not the case. When I started working with automating processes in Photoshop, it was easier to view how others had put their actions together first rather than attempt to create my own. From the feedback I receive on the subject, I'm not the only person who finds this to be true. Some people need a visual reference to make things click, rather than step-by-step text instructions. That is why this chapter covers using actions, and Chapter 3 covers creating actions. If you want to jump right into building actions, I suggest you move straight to Chapter 3 and then return here to learn how to modify your creations.

2

Chapter Contents

Loading Actions

As discussed, actions are excellent tools for shaving time off repetitive tasks or applying past tricks to new images, but they don't do much good unless you can get them into Photoshop and play them.

You can load actions into the Actions palette when the palette is in either Button or List mode. To load an action set (this is what actually occurs, as actions are saved in sets), follow these steps:

1. Open the Actions palette menu.

2. Choose Load Actions from the menu.

3. Browse to the action set on your hard drive that you want to load.

4. Highlight the correct set, and click Load.

If the action you are looking for resides in the Presets\Photoshop Actions folder in the Adobe Photoshop subfolder, the action set appears at the bottom of the Actions palette menu. Simply open the menu, and select that action set from the list (see Figure 2.1).

Figure 2.1 Action sets saved in the Presets\Photoshop Actions folder appear at the bottom of the Actions palette menu.

If, like me, you eventually become addicted to these little scripts and decide to build a library of actions that you create and also acquire from third-party sources online or elsewhere (see Chapter 4 for a listing of online action resources), I recommend that you not save these to the Adobe Photoshop\Presets\Photoshop Actions folder but in another folder.

Note: In Photoshop 7 and earlier versions of the software, the palette menu can become unavailable if too many action sets are saved to the Photoshop Actions folder in the Adobe Photoshop subfolder. This problem seems to have been corrected in Photoshop CS. If you encounter this problem, simply removing the extra action sets from the Photoshop Actions folder corrects it.

Beyond the warning just given, I've discovered another downside to installing far too many actions. Take a look at Figure 2.1 again. See how the action sets are listed in a single column, leaving plenty of room on the desktop? If you save 20 or 30 action sets in that folder, the list appears in two columns, still leaving plenty of room on the desktop. Now take a look at Figure 2.2, with hundreds of actions saved in the `Presets\Photoshop Actions` folder. The Actions palette menu dominates the entire workspace. I work with a dual monitor system, and the excess actually spills over to the other screen.

The other reason I recommend saving additional actions to a folder outside the Photoshop folder is simply for organization. I have thousands of actions on my computer—some from other action fanatics and thousands of my own that run the gamut from simple image correction to melted chrome text effects. With so many varieties, it is simply easier to keep these scripts in a manageable folder system elsewhere on the hard drive. This also makes it easier to find the default or packaged actions that were installed with the software. If you have a smaller hard drive or concerns about clutter, you can load the actions from a CD or from an external drive. Burning large numbers of actions to a CD and then using them with Photoshop is definitely an option. Loading externally saved actions is the same as loading actions from your hard drive, except that you access the CD instead of the hard drive.

Dock to Palette Well	Amulet	Bottle	Conduit	FishTank	HewnStone	Microchip
✓ Button Mode	Animetal	BottledWater	CopperOutline	FlintstoneNotebook	Highlighted	Milky
New Action…	AnotherNeon	BoyHowdy	CopperPlated	Foil	Horizon	Mint
New Set…	AnotherScanLines	Brasso	CorkCarving	FoolsGold	HornetNest	MisterLee
Duplicate	AO	Brian	Corrode	FormedLeather	HornetStorm	Mistique
Delete	Aquaduct	Bronze	CorruptFlesh	Frames	HotMetal	MoneyStacks
Play	Arsenal	BrushedBorder1	CorruptSteel	Frames	HotWires	Moody
	Aztek	BrushedBorder2	CrystalizedBorder	Frazzled	Humdeedum	MosaicBorder
Start Recording	Bammer	BrushedBorder3	Currency	FromWhence	Hyperdrive	Mossy
Record Again	Basics1	BugsGotIt	DanteText	FrostyBorder	ICY	Motherboard
Insert Menu Item…	Basics10	ButterMelt	DeadlyText	FruitJuice	Image Effects	Mothership
Insert Stop…	Basics2	ButterMilk	DecayedText	FunkyMusic	Image Effects	NeedMorePaint
Insert Path	Basics3	Cabinet	DeepBlue	Funzies	ImpliedButton	Nevermore
Action Options…	Basics4	Camoflage	DeepEnd	FutureCartoons	InstantLogo	NexusPrime
Playback Options…	Basics5	Candles	DeepWater	FutureFont	IxNay	NightSwim
	Basics6	CandleWax	Delicate	Galvanized	JaggedRaisedBorder	Nuggets
Clear All Actions	Basics7	Carnival	DepthNeon	Ghastly	Jax	OakInlay
Reset Actions	Basics8	CarnivalAtNight	DepthsOfSpace	GildedNamePlate	JAZZembed	Observe
Load Actions…	Basics9	Carving	Desert	GlamRock	Jeepers	OceanRipple
Replace Actions…	BasicStone	CarvingDark	DigitalCandy	GlowDots	JukeBox	OldMirrors
Save Actions…	BathWater	CashShredder	DigitalFlowers	GlowStone	JukeBoxBackdropped	OnesAndZeros
	BattleGroup	CellScanner	Dizzy	GlyphTablet	Jungle	Oranges
101	BeatenBronze	CelticRomance	DoubleBevelFrame	Gold_Marble_Inlay	JustLoud	OtherSplat
3DimensionalText	BeatenBronzeLight	CelticSwirl	Dunbarden	GoldDust	Kilt	Outland
4Buttons	Bedrock	CenterCut	DwarvenDagger	GoldInDarkness	LED1	outlines
4thDimensionFlux	BeekerStorms	ChickenScratch	DwarvenGems	GoodTime	LensFrame	Outstanding
A_Screw	BeforeThePool	ChipSet	EARTH	GrainedWood	Lettermans	PaintedSands
AbbyPastel	BeforeThePoolAtNight	ChizelBoy	EarthCore	GraniteMoss	LicencePlate	PainterOops
ActionFx_Colored_Text	BetweenTheLines	ChromeDynamo	Earthen	GrapeFruit	LizardHideFrame	Paneling
ActionFx_fancy_borders	BetweenTheLinesDark	ChromeMaster	Eclectic	Graphoid	LunarCarved	PaperBack1
ActionFxPhotoEffects	BeyondFrame	Cigar	EggShell	GraphoidOnBlack	LunarText	Patina1
ActionNeon	BigCity	CircuitStorm	ElChromo	Graved	Mars	Patina2
AFX-CRYSTAL	BigRed	Citrus	EmeraldSteel	GrimmJack	MatrixArt	Patriots
AlienGotHim	Biopsy	CloudsWithMuscle	Excavate	Gum	Max	Phase
Al's Killer Metal Text	BlackStar	CloudyBorders	ExperimentInWatercolors	GunMetal	MaxOnBlack	PhaseDark
AM	BlueStone	Commands	ExtrudePhoto	HappyGretchen	Mesh	Piping
	Boldend	Commands	FancyCutout	Hatched	Metal_In_Motion	PittedChrome
	BoldMetal	Concrete	FancyPhotoback1	Hatchet	MetalPlayground	PixelBorder
	BorgSynapsis	Conduct	FireStorm	Headlights	Meticullus	Pixeldots

Figure 2.2 Saving too many action sets to the `Presets\Photoshop Actions` folder results in the palette menu dominating the workspace.

To load action sets, follow these simple steps:

1. From the Actions palette menu, choose Load Actions to open the Load dialog box, which is shown in Figure 2.3.

Figure 2.3 Find the action set you want to load on your hard drive or CD-ROM.

2. Select the action set and click Load.
    The action set is now available for use in the Actions palette (see Figure 2.4).

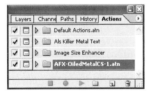

Figure 2.4 Clicking the Load button makes the highlighted action set available for use in the Actions palette.

Saving Actions

After you create an action or a series of actions (learn about creating custom actions in the next chapter) or edit one to fit your needs, you'll want to save it to your hard drive and perhaps later place your actions on a CD.

To save actions, follow these steps:

1. Select the action set where your action or actions reside (see Figure 2.5).

2. Open the Actions palette menu and choose Save Actions from the list (see Figure 2.6).

Figure 2.5 The action set must be selected for the Save Actions option to be available.

Figure 2.6 Choose Save Actions from the palette menu.

3. Find the folder in which you want to save the action or action set, and click OK.

Playing Actions

When an action is in the Actions palette, playing the action is a piece of cake. Once you get over the hurdle of distinguishing between action sets (which cannot be played) and actions, you'll never forget the process; it's sort of like learning to plug the toaster in to make toast.

Playing an action tells Photoshop to execute a series of prerecorded commands specific to the action. If the action has a modal control, you can specify the values for that when the action pauses and the dialog box for that control opens.

Actions play the same whether the palette is in List or Button mode, although the process for starting play is slightly different. Also, you have more control over the action (which commands are played) in List mode.

Playing Actions: Button Mode

To play an action while the Actions palette is in Button mode, you must first know whether the action needs an open file/photograph or whether the action creates its own document (as with many text and special effects actions). For this example I'm going to demonstrate running a text action that creates its own document. I'm using the action that I placed in the palette in the "Loading Actions" section, called AFX-OiledMetalCS-1, which is available on the CD in the Chapter 2 folder (see Figure 2.7).

Vignette (selection)	Frame Channel - 50 ...	Wood Frame - 50 pixel
Cast Shadow (type)	Water Reflection (ty...	Custom RGB to Gray...
Molten Lead	Make Clip Path (sele...	Sepia Toning (layer)
Quadrant Colors	Save As Photoshop ...	Gradient Map
Action 1	Image Sharpening 1	Image Sharpening 2
Image Sharpening 3	Image Sharpening 4	Image Sharpening 5
AFX-OiledMetalCS-1		

Figure 2.7 The Actions palette in Button mode: the action AFX-OiledMetalCS-1 is at the bottom left of the palette.

To play the action, simply click the corresponding button in the Actions palette. For this particular action, a message in the form of a Stop appears immediately when you click the button, informing the user that this action creates its own document (see Figure 2.8).

Figure 2.8 Some Stop messages simply provide information about the action.

Both the Continue and the Stop button are available. The person recording an action can cause a hard stop or allow the user to continue with no action taken. Since this message is simply for information, no action is required. Click Continue to proceed with the playback process.

During the course of the action, you might be asked to change a setting or insert text, as with the Stop in Figure 2.9. In this instance, only a Stop button is available. When you click the Stop button, the action expects you to carry out the requested step as outlined in the message. When you meet those requirements, you can continue running the action by clicking the Play Selection button at the bottom of the palette again. If you follow the directions carefully as given by the action and continue running through to completion, you should receive results similar if not identical to those achieved when the action was recorded (see Figure 2.10).

Figure 2.9 Stops can be used to instruct the user to perform a specific function at a given point during playback.

Figure 2.10 When `AFX-OiledMetalCS-1.atn` is played back successfully, it gives you reflective metal text.

Button mode is great, providing you don't need to adjust the action itself. Button mode is quick, easy, and well organized—perfect if you like a little order to your desktop.

Playing Actions: List Mode

To play actions while the Actions palette is in List mode, you have a couple of options. The primary thing to keep in mind is the difference between an action set and an action: if the action set is selected, the option to play is not available. An action within a set must be selected in order to play anything. This may seem redundant, but this mistake is actually quite prevalent among those just starting with actions. In Figure 2.11, an action set (AFX-CloudsOverWaterCS) is selected. Note that the Stop, Record, and Play buttons at the bottom of the palette are grayed out. Opening the Actions palette menu will reveal that the play function there is not available as well.

Figure 2.11 Actions cannot be played if an action set is selected.

Selecting an action within the set (see Figure 2.12) makes the control buttons for the action available. Also, the Play function returns in the Actions palette menu.

Figure 2.12 Selecting an action within a set gives control over the action back to the user.

To play an action in List mode, follow these steps:

1. Load an action set into the Actions palette (if the action set is not already resident in the palette).

2. Expand the action set containing the action you want to play.

3. In the Actions palette, select the action you want to play.

4. You can now play the action in one of three ways:

- Click the Play Selection button at the bottom of the Actions palette (see Figure 2.13).

- Open the Actions palette menu and click Play.

- If the action has a shortcut key assignment, press that combination.

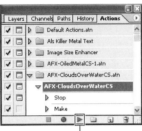

Play Selection

Figure 2.13 Clicking the Play Selection button plays the selected action when the Actions palette is in List mode.

To demonstrate how easy this really is, load the action set AFX-CloudsOver-WaterCS found on the CD in the Chapter 2 folder. This action creates its own document, so do not be concerned about having a photo open. Now follow these steps:

1. Expand the CloudsOverWaterCS action set.

2. Select the action CloudsOverWaterCS.

3. Click the Play Selection button at the bottom of the Actions palette.

4. Carefully follow the directions that appear. In this particular action, the only command that you need really be concerned about is entering the text with the Type Mask tool, instead of the standard Type tool. The Type Mask tool appears as a capital *T* made of dotted lines ⛶, or "marching ants." When this command appears, be sure to use a large font size as requested in the Stop message (see Figure 2.14).

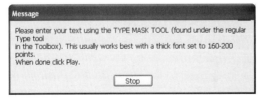

Figure 2.14 In order for the action to run properly, follow the Stop messages carefully.

5. After you meet the conditions in the Stop message, click the Play Selection button again (found at the bottom of the palette).

6. The action should play through to completion to the final Stop message (see Figure 2.15). Click OK.

Figure 2.15 A final Stop message can display information about the action or designer and even advertise.

Your new document should have created text that appears to be filled with cloudy variations between white and blue, with a rough outline around the text (see Figure 2.16).

Figure 2.16 If an action has performed as expected, the results should be nearly identical to those seen when it was first recorded.

Note: To see the color version of the image created by this action, check the color section of this book. It is also on the CD in the Chapter 2 folder, as `cloudyText.psd`.

If you have made it this far with a decent understanding of how to load and play actions, you have mastered a large part of the learning curve attached to actions. Something as seemingly simple as loading and playing these scripts stops many people in their tracks. Just remember: large meals are conquered in small, bite-sized pieces.

Editing Actions

If you are wondering why this section on editing actions comes before the section on recording actions, which is covered in Chapter 3, let me explain.

In my experience, I've found that people learning actions for the first time often attempt to conform an existing action to their particular need. Most people use prerecorded actions made by other people before creating their own. That's why I teach actions in this order and why I'm structuring the book in this way. Demonstrating editing actions on an existing action is simply easier than going through the recording process and then doing the editing. When we reach that point in Chapter 3, I'll review how to edit your own actions.

 Note: You can edit actions only with the Actions palette in List mode.

With actions, nothing is written in stone; you can add to them or subtract from them, rearrange the order of commands within an action, or even add commands from other actions. You might want to edit an action for any of several reasons:

- To turn commands on and off
- To adjust the recorded settings so that the action plays with the new settings each time
- To duplicate commands
- To tell the action to ask for your input each time on the commands you specify
- To rearrange the position of commands within the action
- To record or delete new commands
- To delete commands entirely
- To change options assigned to the action, such as name, shortcut keys, color designation, and playback options (speed of playback, pause for audio annotation)
- To include commands copied from other actions

Turning Commands On and Off

Commands within an action can be toggled on or off, giving you the option to play each command or bypass recorded commands within the action during playback. To turn commands on and off, you need only check or uncheck the Toggle Item On/Off check box corresponding to the command on the left side of the Actions palette. Figure 2.17 shows an expanded action with all commands toggled on and then shows the same action with the Invert and Convert Mode commands toggled off.

 Note: If you want to run an action several times, but it has a Stop describing what the action does, you might not want the action to stop and display the message each time it is played. Read it once, and then toggle the Stop off.

Figure 2.17 Unchecking the Toggle Item On/Off check boxes tells the action to bypass the command during playback. In (a) all commands are toggled on; in (b) two commands are toggled off.

The ability to toggle commands on and off is helpful if actions perform more than one task. Let's say you have a single action that converts an image to grayscale, reduces the image to thumbnail size, and saves the image at a reduced resolution to a new folder for use on a web page or photo gallery. Perhaps after the web page is designed, you decide that the thumbnails need not be gray but would look better in color. Rather than deleting the command entirely (you might want other thumbnails to be gray in the future), you can simply toggle the command that does the grayscale conversion off so that when the action is played on a new image, the color is retained but the size is still reduced and the image saved as before.

Here's something to keep in mind, especially when working with actions that have commands that look for specific conditions carried out earlier in the same action. If you toggle a command off, and the action later tries to perform a function that is based on the conditions met by that command (such as the renaming of a layer), either the action will stop and display an error message, or the end result may be quite different from what you expect.

For instance, let's say at the beginning of the action, you record a step that duplicates the Background layer. The new layer is called Background Copy by default. For the remainder of the action, the steps interact with the Background Copy layer in some way. If you toggle off the step that copies the Background layer and then play the action, you will receive error messages every time the action tries to find the Background Copy layer, as none is created. Chapter 3 covers problems such as this in the section on troubleshooting.

Editing Commands in the Action

Omitting or including commands in an action is as simple as toggling the commands on or off. Between the Toggle Item On/Off check boxes and the actions command list is a series of boxes. These represent commands that have dialog boxes attached to the command, wherein the settings can be changed. Figure 2.18 shows the modal controls (Toggle Dialog On/Off) for the dialog boxes.

Figure 2.18 Dialog boxes attached to commands may open with the modal control on (box filled). When the modal control is off, the command applies the original setting.

You can edit commands with attached dialog boxes when the modal control corresponding to the command is filled with a miniature representation of a dialog box. This causes the dialog box for that command to appear at that stage in the action where the settings for that command can be changed or accepted. You can accept the default settings, or settings that were originally recorded in the action, each time by unchecking the modal control.

For example, load the action set AFX-SketchesCS-1.atn. I'll demonstrate using the photo 0770143_HIGH.jpg, supplied by Photospin.com (see Figure 2.19).

Figure 2.19 Image of a praying woman, supplied by Photospin.com

1. With AFX-SketchesCS-1.atn action set loaded into the Actions palette, expand the set and select AFX-PencilSketch, the topmost of two actions in the set.

2. Turn off the modal controls for all commands with attached dialog boxes (see Figure 2.20).

3. Play the action.

Figure 2.20 With modal controls turned off, the action will run through to completion, provided there are no errors, without asking for user input.

When this action has run through to completion, you will have an image that appears to be a pencil drawing made with soft strokes, as in Figure 2.21. You can alter the end result by having the dialog boxes open and check or edit the settings for each. Give that a try now.

Figure 2.21 Result of the action AFX-PencilSketch

Open the History palette and click the image icon at the top to return the document to its original state.

2. Select the action AFX-PencilSketch once again.

3. Turn on the modal controls for each command, as shown in Figure 2.22.

Figure 2.22 The AFX-PencilSketch action, but with the modal controls turned on in the Actions palette

4. Rerun the action.

5. When the Duplicate Layer dialog box opens, click OK to accept it.

6. When the Layer Styles/Blending Options dialog box opens, make no changes and click OK.

7. The Gaussian Blur dialog box opens. For this particular effect, the amount of Gaussian Blur applied to the layer the action has selected dictates the strength or the darkness of the pencil effect. By adjusting the amount of Gaussian Blur, as I've done in Figure 2.23 by increasing the blur radius to 250 pixels, I can darken the detail and shadow of the sketch.

Rerecording Commands

You have seen how to alter the results of an action by displaying the dialog boxes. Although this can be helpful, it's also tedious if you plan to use the action multiple times. Another option is to edit a command once, effectively recording that step again, and then saving the action with the new setting.

I'll demonstrate using the same action as before, AFX-PencilSketch. Let's say I want to permanently change the Gaussian Blur command so that each time this action is run, the result is the darker version of the pencil sketch. Here's one way to do it:

1. Turn off the modal controls for the action (as shown earlier in Figure 2.20).

2. Open the Actions palette menu and select Playback Options from the list.

3. In the Playback Options dialog box, check Pause For and enter a value of 2 or 3 seconds (see Figure 2.24).

4. Click OK.

Figure 2.23 By adjusting the Gaussian Blur settings, the image results in a darker, more detailed sketch.

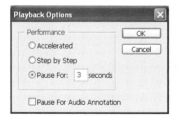

Figure 2.24 You can pause the playback for the action so that you can edit the appropriate command during playback.

5. Open the original photo again, select the action, and click the Play button.

6. When the action reaches the Gaussian Blur step, click Stop at the bottom of the palette. Enter the new Gaussian Blur setting.

7. Click Play again, running the action to completion. You can stop at this point if you choose or finish the action as recorded.

8. Save the action set with a new name.

Saving the action set with a new name gives you another instance of the line art effect: now both versions are saved.

If you already know the new setting for the command you want to change, you can simply double-click that command in the action without running the action, change the settings in the corresponding dialog box, and click OK. The action records the change without your having to walk through every step. Keep in mind that this only works for those commands with dialog boxes.

Rearranging Commands

You can alter the order in which commands and steps execute. To do so, click the command you want to move (see Figure 2.25) and drag it to where you want the command to execute during playback.

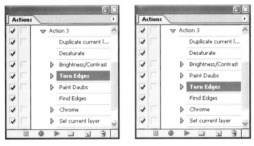

Figure 2.25 Select the command you want to move, and drag it to the new position in the commands list.

You want to be certain the command you are moving does not affect the following steps in the action. For instance, applying a filter at a different time in an action may not stop the flow of commands during playback. A command that changes the name of a layer that later has commands applied to it may result in an error. Again, the Chapter 3 section on troubleshooting will discuss these pitfalls.

Adding Steps

You can add steps to an action anywhere within the action by simply recording them at the point where you want to inject a new step.

For example, load the action set AFX-RumpledSatin.atn (found in the Chapter 2 folder on the CD) and play the action through to completion, being careful to follow the Stop messages. Figure 2.26 shows the end result of this action as recorded.

Figure 2.26 The result of AFX-RumpledSatin.atn. You can see this image to its full effect in the the color section.

I like the action, but adding a few steps will vary the effect, often rendering completely different results. To add to this action, follow these steps:

1. Select the last command performed just prior to the final Stop message and click the Record button (see Figure 2.27).

Record

Figure 2.27 Begin recording after the last command prior to the final Stop message.

2. Record additional commands by simply manipulating the current image. For instance, adjust the Brightness/Contrast or apply a filter.

3. Stop recording (see Figure 2.28).

Figure 2.28 When you finish adding effects, stop recording.

4. Save the new recording as a new action and/or action set (see Figure 2.29).

Figure 2.29 Rename and save the new action/action set.

Figure 2.30 shows the results of the new action created by adding additional steps to the action. The layered .psd file for this image is in the Chapter 2 folder of the CD (wildStripes.psd), as well as the new action set AFX-WildStripes.atn.

Figure 2.30 The resulting type effect from the new action. This example is also in the color section.

Deleting Steps

At times, you might want to erase a command from an action entirely. For instance, when I'm working with photo effects involving blending mode changes to layers, I'll cycle through a few blending modes while the action is recording until I find the mode that gives me the mix I want. The action recorded all those changes, whereas only the final blending mode change is required. These steps make clutter and increase processing time and can be removed without harming the action or its result.

To delete a step or a command from an action, select the item in the Actions palette (see Figure 2.31) and drag it to the trashcan button at the bottom of the Actions palette.

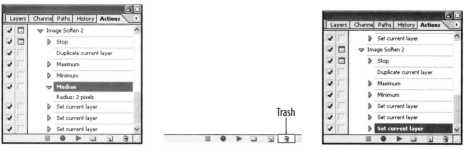

Figure 2.31 Select the command you want to remove from the action, and drag it to the palette trash.

You can also delete a command by activating it, opening the Actions palette menu, and choosing Delete.

Duplicating Commands

To duplicate a command or a step in an action, first highlight the item in the Actions palette (see Figure 2.32) and then drag the command to the Create New Action button. Rather than create a new action, Photoshop duplicates the command, placing it directly beneath the original.

Figure 2.32 Select the command in the action that you want to duplicate, and drag it to the Create New Action button.

You can also duplicate a command by activating it from the list in the Actions palette, opening the Actions palette menu, and choosing Duplicate.

Adding Commands from Other Actions

Though I think you will find it doesn't happen frequently, you can add commands from one action to another. Say, for instance, you have a pair of actions that each perform different image-correction functions. For the second action, you recorded a Save For Web step to decrease the file size (see Figure 2.33) You want to apply those same settings to the first action.

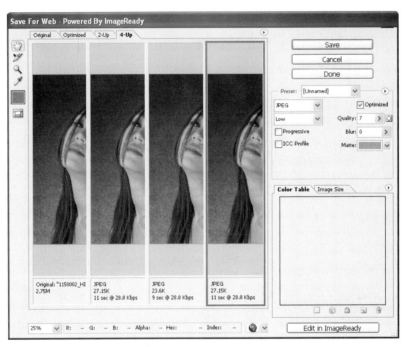

Figure 2.33 The Save For Web dialog box

To add a command from one action to another:

1. Be sure that both actions are in the Actions palette. They need not reside in the same set.

2. Select the command you want to add to the other action in the action where it currently resides (see Figure 2.34).

3. Duplicate the command, as in the preceding section.

4. Drag and drop the duplicate command to the other action, placing it in the list where you want the command to take place. In this case, because it is saving the file after the correction has been performed, place the command at the end of the command string.

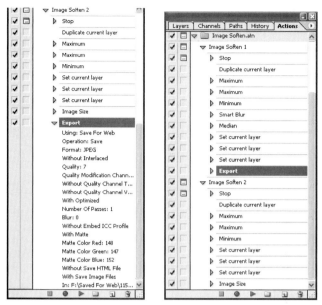

Figure 2.34 Select the command, duplicate it, and drag the duplicate into position in the second action.

Playback Options

The ability to control an action's playback speed is particularly useful when troubleshooting an action. You use items in the Playback Options dialog box, which is accessed from the Actions palette menu, to alter the pause between commands:

Accelerated (**Normal Speed, Default**) The action plays without pausing and without allowing you to see the commands being performed on the image.

Step By Step The action is still fast, but this option lets you see each command being applied to the image.

Pause For This options inserts a timed pause between commands, allowing you to set the speed. Even a one-second delay can slow long actions to the point that playback is unbearable, so use with caution. This setting is primarily for troubleshooting purposes, but is also helpful when trying to learn the techniques applied in third-party actions (as shown earlier in Figure 2.24).

Pause For Audio Annotation Actions can include audio annotation. If such is attached to the action, you can use this setting to pause the action for audio playback, or you can leave it unchecked to bypass any audio messages.

When adjusting the Playback Options setting, all actions are affected and will pause or not pause until the Playback Options are changed again.

The Action Options Tool

This tool primarily allows you to name the action, assign it a color for organization when in Button mode, and assign a shortcut key combination to run the action. You can alter these options by double-clicking the action name in the Actions palette or by selecting Action Options from the palette menu.

The naming convention, shortcut keys, and color coding are left to your discretion; you will know how best to keep track of the actions you create or modify. What I will point out is that you have 60 shortcut key combinations available to you, using combinations of the function keys, Shift, and Command/Ctrl (see Figure 2.35).

Figure 2.35 You can name, colorize, and assign shortcut key combinations to the action via the Action Options dialog box.

Creating and Using Actions

3

I hope by now you are beginning to get a few ideas about how actions can help you streamline your day-to-day image editing and correction. This chapter covers the creation of actions from scratch, start to finish. You will also learn how to use actions to batch process entire folders of images, reducing your workload and decreasing production time.

Chapter Contents

Recording an Action: From Start to Finish

So what is the best way, the most effective way, to teach a person how to create actions? I find that the best way is to walk them through the process, step by step, and that is exactly what I intend to do in this section. I will walk you through not only creating the action, but through every step I record along the way. When we're done, you should be able to record and save your own actions and have a pretty cool sharpening technique at your disposal.

Note: Before getting started, remember what you learned from the first chapter about items that can and cannot be recorded in actions. As you work with them more, what you can tell your actions to accomplish will become intuitive; keeping the list close at hand while getting started will prevent a lot of frustration during the learning curve.

Stage 1: Setting Up Photoshop to Begin Recording a New Action

What is the best way to get your feet wet and begin recording actions? I'd wager you can approach the process in the same manner you might begin learning in a classroom environment. Before the lessons even begin, a few things need to be in order. A fresh notebook, a clean desktop, and an eager attitude to learn are essential. When approaching Photoshop with the master plan to learn actions, the mouse or tablet will serve as your pencil and the workspace as your notebook (as yet free of notes and doodles). That leaves a workspace free of excess clutter. We'll take care of that now.

Before jumping in to the following steps, which will require you to wipe away all the actions currently residing in the palette, ensure that any actions in the palette that have been recorded, altered, or otherwise edited to your specifications have been saved. Also, remember that if you have an edited action in the palette, effectively creating a new result from an existing action, save that action set under a new name so that the original is not overwritten. You might want to review the section on saving actions before proceeding with the following steps.

Note: If your action will be run on images of different sizes or dimensions, change the ruler units to percent before recording the action. When you do so, the commands in the action that are modal specific will play back in the same general area in each image.

1. Clear all the actions from the Actions palette. This will avoid confusion when you look at the finished action later. To clear all actions and action sets, open the Actions palette menu and choose Clear All Actions.

2. Open an image that could use some sharpening. For this example, I'm using a photo of a young lady supplied by my friends at PhotoSpin.com. You can find the image, titled `sweetgirl.jpg`, on the companion CD (see Figure 3.1). The image I'm using already looks pretty clear, doesn't it? But just wait until I'm done with it. If you can't see a stark change, I'll eat my proverbial hat. The effect will be that of adding age to the photo, at least to a degree; the lines and features should appear sharper at the end as well.

Figure 3.1 Photo of a young lady

3. Actions must be placed in sets, so create an action set by clicking the Create New Set button at the bottom of the Actions palette. It looks like a file folder. In the Set Options dialog box, name the set Image Sharpening Techniques, as shown in Figure 3.2. Click OK.

Figure 3.2 Name the new set in the Set Options dialog box.

4. Click the Create New Action button at the bottom of the Actions palette, immediately to the right of the Create New Set button and to the left of the Trash button. It looks to be a piece of paper with the lower-left corner folded.

 Note: If you recorded an Open Image command, the action would attempt to open the same image every time.

5. In the New Action dialog box:
    *   Name the action Image Sharpening 1 (just in case you want to place more sharpening actions in the set at a later date).
    *   The set for the action will be the one just created: Image_Sharpening.atn.
    *   Assign a function key combination of Command/Control+Shift+F7.
    *   Change the Color option to Gray (see Figure 3.3).

Figure 3.3 Set the action options before recording the action.

6. Click Record. Every function performed in Photoshop beyond this point is recorded into the action until you click Stop.

Take a look at the Actions palette. You will have your set, the new action, and the Record button at the bottom is pressed, indicating that Photoshop is in record mode (see Figure 3.4).

Figure 3.4 The current state of the Actions palette

Stage 2: Recording the Technique

As I approached this section, I considered simply teaching you to record quick actions with minimal steps. But I decided against this is because I want you to see that actions can be used for more than simple shortcuts. Actions are excellent for performing advanced techniques as well.

The point to the following process is not to demonstrate the perfect sharpening technique. The point is to demonstrate Photoshop's ability to record extended actions with multiple steps. Please don't think that this action demonstrates how images should be sharpened in every instance or even most instances. What I want you to take away from this is that you will have a functioning action that follows the exact same steps, in order, every time you run it. Images will vary, and the requirements for correcting them will vary. Unless the action is edited, it will follow the exact same procedure every time, regardless of the image requirements.

1. In the Layers palette, duplicate the Background layer twice. By default, the new layers will be named Background Copy and Background Copy 2.

2. With the Background Copy 2 layer selected, choose Filter > Blur > Gaussian Blur. Set the radius of the blur to 3 pixels (see Figure 3.5) and click OK.

Figure 3.5 Adding some Gaussian Blur

3. Duplicate the Background Copy 2 layer, creating a new layer called Background Copy 3. Choose Filter > Gaussian Blur and again apply a 3-pixel blur to the Background Copy 3 layer.

 Note: Both of those Filter menu commands are correct. When you use a filter, it appears at the top of the filter list as its own item for repeat use.

4. With the Background Copy 3 layer still selected, choose Image > Adjustments > Invert. Immediately following, choose Image > Adjustments > Desaturate. Figure 3.6 shows the current state of the image. (Some of these steps may seem strange, but bear with me. Step 4 helps reduce the amount of "halo" created by a step to be recorded further in the action.)

Figure 3.6 The current state of the image

5. I'm going to seriously bump up the contrast of the black-and-white layer by using levels. Choose Image > Adjustments > Levels, and apply settings close to those shown in Figure 3.7: shadow 111, midpoint 0.92, highlight 242. Again, this layer will help eliminate some contrasty halos in a future step.

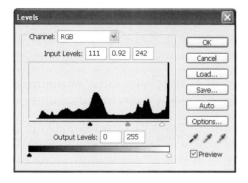

Figure 3.7 Increase the contrast of the Background Copy 3 layer by applying these Levels settings.

6. Change the blending mode of the Background Copy 3 layer to Overlay.

7. Select the Background Copy 2 layer. Change the blending mode for this layer to Overlay as well (see Figure 3.8).

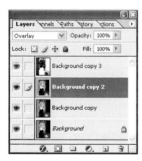

Figure 3.8 Change the blending mode to Overlay for both top layers.

8. Desaturate the Background Copy 2 layer. The image appears a bit sharper already (see Figure 3.9).

9. Select the Background Copy 3 layer, and reduce the layer's opacity to 50%.

10. Select the Background Copy 2 layer, and set the opacity to 70% (see Figure 3.10).

11. Rather than setting both top layers to Overlay, I'm thinking that one could be set to Soft Light to reduce the amount of contrast just a bit. Select the Background Copy 3 layer, and change the blending mode to Soft Light.

Figure 3.9 Some sharpening appears

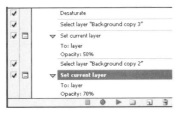

Figure 3.10 Commands as they're being recorded in the Actions palette

12. Now that the image is tweaked to handle the unnatural halo that the next step creates, we can record the step that will act as our sharpening agent. Select the Background Copy layer and duplicate it. This creates a new layer, Background Copy 4, placed just above the Background Copy layer. Set the blending mode for the new layer to Soft Light (see Figure 3.11).

Figure 3.11 Set up a new layer on which the sharpening will take place.

13. Choose Filter > Other > High Pass (see Figure 3.12). Enter a radius of 40 pixels and click OK.

Figure 3.12 The High Pass filter in action (no pun intended)

14. Stop recording by clicking the Stop icon at the bottom of the Actions palette. The final image will appear reasonably sharper than the original, without loss of quality by increased harmonics that the High Pass filter often causes when steps are not taken to correct it (see Figure 3.13).

Figure 3.13 Detail enhanced with this simple process

I believe it was important to demonstrate the recording of actions using a long process to emphasize the power behind these scripts. You now have an action that will sharpen any image you care to run the action on, simply by selecting the action and clicking the Play button while in List mode or by clicking the button/using the shortcut key combination weighing in Button mode.

Granted, this may not produce quality results on every image, but the focus here was to demonstrate the creation of an action and not the end result for every image. Often actions are image or image-type specific. Please keep in mind that no action is a cure all in every situation.

Figure 3.14 shows how your Actions palette should now appear. Figure 3.15 displays before and after shots of sweetgirl.jpg. Quite a contrast between the two images, wouldn't you say?

Before I begin receiving e-mails on the strength or weakness of this sharpening method, let me provide this disclaimer. Using Photoshop, you can sharpen images in dozens, if not hundreds, of ways, of which this is only one variation.

Figure 3.14 The current state of the Actions palette

Figure 3.15 Contrasting the before (left) and after (right) shots

Stage 3: Saving the Action

It's time to save your custom action. To do so, follow these steps:

1. Select the action set (see Figure 3.16). You must select the set, not the actions, or you will not be able to save.

Figure 3.16 To save the action, you must select the action set.

2. Open the Actions palette menu and choose Save Actions.

3. Find the folder in which you want to save the action (see Figure 3.17).

4. Click Save.

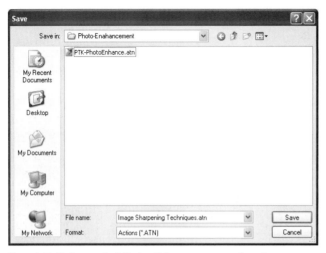

Figure 3.17 Navigate to the folder in which you want to save the action.

If you're not happy with the name of your action set, you can change it in one of two ways. You can double-click the action set in the Actions palette and type the new name, or you can select the action set and, from the Actions palette menu, choose Set Options to open the Set Options dialog box and rename the action set. After you enter the new name, click OK. If you want to save the action set with the new name, you will have to go through the save process again.

 Note: Rename the set to something that will help you remember what types of actions the set contains, for ease of locating an effect at a later date.

Take a look at the action that was just recorded one more time. First, open the Actions palette menu and change the mode to Button. The Actions palette should now display a single gray action button called Sharpening - 1, with a shortcut key combination of Shft+F7 (see Figure 3.18).

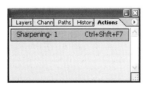

Figure 3.18 The action with the palette in Button mode. Note the name, color, and shortcut key combination

Stage 4: Testing the Action on Other Images

Part of the recording process, a vital part, is testing the actions after you create them. I'm going to rerun the action on a new photograph. Figure 3.19 shows the photograph before the action test and the photograph after using the action to apply the sharpening technique.

Figure 3.19 Test Subject Number One, before (left) and after (right) the action (Photo supplied by PhotoSpin.com.)

What would happen if you performed this action on an image other than the photograph of a person? Another test is in order. Figure 3.20 shows the test image: a large rusty piece of metal (rustyMetal.jpg, found on the CD) with some bold text raised from the surface, alongside results of the action test on the metal test subject. Not only is the character of the metal sharpened, but the corrosion is enhanced as well. With the action saved to the hard drive, it can now be loaded into the Actions palette at a future date or tied to a batch command (or Droplet) and run on multiple images. (Batch processing will be covered later in this chapter.)

Figure 3.20 Subject photo for the second test: finding out how this action will affect the photo of an object rather than a person (Photo supplied by PhotoSpin.com.)

Stops

Stop messages are pop-up dialog boxes that you can insert directly into an action to deliver short bits of information to the user. You can use them for several purposes: giving directions to yourself or another user to perform some task before continuing the action, describing what the action was recorded to do and what the intended result should be, or simply advertising the work or website of the creator.

I generate many type effects that rely on the Type Mask tool in order for the actions to function properly, and as such often remind users of my actions to ensure that the proper type tool is used and the size of the font is correct before proceeding. I often mention characteristics of the font that should be present. (Thick fonts perform best in my work; script fonts as a rule do not.) Stop messages allow me to relay all types of information every time the action is played, including a mini-advertisement for my website.

The options available to you with Stops are basic at best. You can include Stops when you first record the action, or you can insert them later.

Let's take a look at creating Stop messages for the action created in the previous tutorial. To insert a Stop at the beginning of the action after the action has been recorded, you will need to do some rearranging, as you will soon see.

1. Select the action name in the Actions palette.

2. Open the Actions palette menu and choose Insert Stop to open the Record Stop dialog box.

3. Type your message. If the Stop is simply to relay information about the actions (who made it and why, for example), with no steps required of the user, check the Allow Continue check box on the bottom left. This will give the user the option to either stop the action when the message appears during playback or simply continue the action after the message is displayed (see Figure 3.21). Click OK.

Figure 3.21 A check in the Allow Continue check box lets users of the action continue past the Stop by clicking a Continue button when the Stop message appears.

4. When you create a Stop after the action is recorded, it appears at the bottom of the action (see Figure 3.22). Click the Stop and drag it into position at the top of the action.

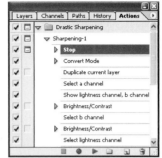

Figure 3.22 After recording the stop for placement at the top of the action, it appears at the bottom of the action as the last command and must be manually moved (left). Drag it to the point in the action where you would like the Stop to appear (right).

If the Stop asks the user to perform some specific function during playback, and they should do so before they proceed, clear the Allow Continue check box. This stops the action during playback; the user can complete the requested step and click the Play button again to restart the action from that point (see Figure 3.23).

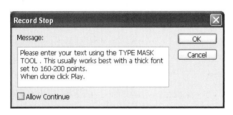

Figure 3.23 Clearing the Allow Continue check box stops the action completely; the user must start the action again after the requested step is performed by clicking Play again.

5. For actions that are distributed online or for others to use, you can inject a friendly goodbye message or plug for a website into the action via a Stop at the end. You need not check the Allow Continue check box in this case (see Figure 3.24).

Figure 3.24 Stops placed at the end of actions are excellent means to convey thanks to the user, as well as put in a plug for your favorite website.

Figure 3.25 shows a Stop message I've inserted at the beginning of the sharpening action created earlier. Note that both a Continue button and a Stop button are present—the result of checking the Allow Continue check box while recording the Stop.

Figure 3.25 The Stop message with the Continue button available

Figure 3.26 shows a Stop message on playback that does not have the Continue button. Since this Stop occurs at the end of the action playback sequence, no option to continue is needed.

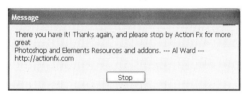

Figure 3.26 The Stop message without the Continue button

Let's take one last look at the action created earlier. Recall the color coding, the naming, the shortcut key combination? All three of these elements come into play when the Actions palette is changed to Button mode. Figure 3.27 shows the state of my loaded actions when the palette is switched to Button mode. Note that the name of the *actions* loaded, not the sets, are shown, along with the key combinations that will play the actions. If you follow a color-coding system to keep track of your actions (what types of functions they perform are good guides for color coding), the buttons will be appropriately hued, providing you applied a color earlier in the Action Options dialog box.

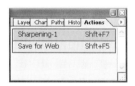

Figure 3.27 The Actions palette in Button mode; name, color coding, and shortcut key combination in place

Teaching Actions to Call Other Actions

Another cool trick that you can program into your action is the ability to call, or play back, another loaded action. You might be wondering, as I was when I first realized that this is possible, why you would want to use an action to play another action. It takes some thought, but this ability lets you squeeze additional power from your actions.

For instance, say you have an action that performs multiple functions on image. When you are done, you would like to save copies of the images to a new folder, to the Web, and so forth. You're not sure how that action will affect images of different color or size. Rather than include a Save command in the action, you can have the action call another action to save the copied images to a specific folder or to play an action with the Save For Web command. This saves time, because you don't need to record the Save command twice (once in the action and once as a separate action). This also helps reduce the number of commands in the Actions palette, reducing clutter and confusion if you are attempting to watch the action playback while in List mode.

Here's an example. Take a look at Figure 3.28. In this capture of the Actions palette, I have the action recorded previously in this chapter and an action that will reduce the size of the images I play the action on for display on the Web. Suppose I would like to call the Save For Web action after the completion of the previous action. Here are the steps I would take to make this happen:

Figure 3.28 Find the spot where you would like to place the command calling another action and click the Record button.

1. Open an image in Photoshop.

2. Ensure that a shortcut key combination has been assigned to the Save For Web action.

3. Click the command in the previous action that will precede the Save For Web action playback. (Again, look at Figure 3.28.)

4. Click the Record button.

5. Press the shortcut key combination assigned to the Save For Web action. You can also include the action in the recording process by double-clicking the Save For Web action, or select it and click Play.

6. Stop Recording.

The playback for this Save For Web action is now recorded in the previous action (see Figure 3.29).

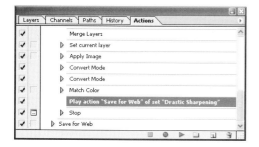

Figure 3.29 You can insert a command to play back another action by using the keyboard shortcuts to play the second action while recording the first.

As you can see, actions can be extremely simple (including a single step) or complex (accessing actions within actions). It takes some thought to automate Photoshop for some of the more advanced corrections or saving functions, but if the process can be recorded, it can be automated. Even those functions that cannot be recorded can be addressed with the Insert Menu Item command or by inserting Stops to allow the user to perform a specific function. At first you will be more comfortable recording the easier processes, and this is to be expected. Keep working with the software, and soon Photoshop will be tackling the extended edits as well.

Batch Processing: From Start to Finish

The real power of actions comes in their ability to be applied to multiple documents in Photoshop or to folders on your hard drive with little or no input from the user. You can do so in two ways: using the Batch command and using Droplets.

Batch processing functions somewhat like an assembly line. In a factory, parts are assembled through a series of repeated steps one at a time until, at the end of the line or production process, a completed product is produced. That product is then packaged, labeled, and shipped to its distribution points. The beauty of an assembly line, as discovered by Ford so long ago, is that identical products can be produced in a relatively short time. This concept brought about the Industrial Revolution and changed the world forever.

The concept behind batch processing is the same. Photoshop allows you to create an action, or a series of commands, that you can use to alter or correct photographs. The Batch command takes that action and applies it to multiple images without the user having to tell Photoshop to run the action each time. Batch processing takes care of this without user input; all that is required is an action and a simple setup via the Batch dialog box.

To open the Batch dialog box (see Figure 3.30), choose File > Automate > Batch.

Note: Before applying the Batch command, ensure that the action that you would like to run on your folders or images is loaded into the Actions palette.

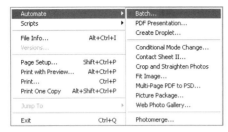

Figure 3.30 To open the Batch dialog box, open the File menu and choose Automate.

As you can see in Figure 3.31, the Batch dialog box is extremely large, and even with your monitor set to a high resolution, it will take up most of your screen and block your view of the current document. Unfortunately, there is really no way around this.

The primary reason this dialog box is so large is to include all the options that you can assign to your batch. The Batch dialog box is divided into four primary areas:

Play Here you can select the set and the action that you want to assign to the Batch command. You must first select the set for the action you want to run and then select the action from that set that you want to run on your images.

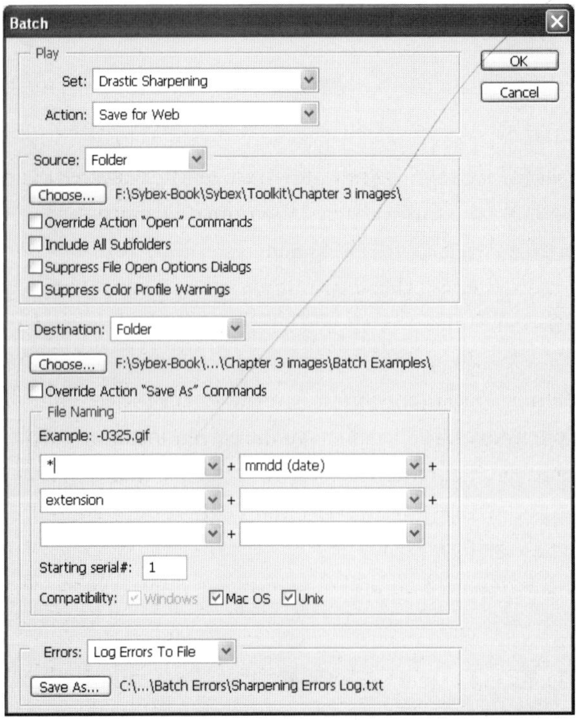

Figure 3.31 The Batch dialog box

Source In this area, you choose which images or folders of images you want to process. You also specify functions you want to override or include in the action during playback.

Destination In this area you set a destination for the images that are to be processed by the Batch command and create a naming convention for those images. You can assign serial numbers, serial letters, and a starting point for your numbering system as well as establish compatibility with other operating systems.

Errors This area concerns errors that could occur during processing. Photoshop can log the errors to a file or stop the batch process completely until you manually clear the problem.

Verbal descriptions are useful but seldom as powerful as simply showing you what I'm talking about. So let's take a look at the separate sections of the Batch dialog box.

The Play area has a faint box around two drop-down menus. From the first menu, you choose the set that contains the action you want to play, and then you choose the action from the next menu. In this example, I selected the Drastic Sharpening set created earlier in this chapter and the Save For Web action that resides within the Drastic Sharpening action set. Unless I've included a step in the Save For Web action that calls another action, this is the only action that will be applied to the images or folders of images that are selected next.

After you select an action, you must tell Photoshop where the images reside that you want to process. Below the Play area is the Source drop-down menu, which contains four items: Folder, Import, Opened Files, and File Browser.

When you select Import as your source, another drop-down menu opens that lists sources from which your computer can import images. PDF Image is one example; I also have the option of using Dual-Mode DSC (2770) as a source.

The Source: File Browser selection is special, in that only those images selected in the File Browser—a single item, multiple images, or every image in a given location—will be processed during the execution of the Batch command. To select multiple images in the File Browser, Command/Ctrl+click each image; *or* flag the desired images (Sort > Flag) and then choose Flagged Files from the Show drop-down in the upper-right corner. To arrange the order in which images are processed, drag-and-drop them in the File Browser.

Note: You can perform many other automation functions from within the File Browser itself, such as Batch Rename (one of the best features in Photoshop, in my humble opinion), Picture Package, Contact Sheet II, PDF Presentation, Web Photo Gallery, and even Photomerge.

If you select Folder as your batch source, click Choose to find the source folder on your computer.

Immediately beneath the Source drop-down and Choose button are four check boxes. When you select Override Action "Open" Commands, you are given the warning shown in Figure 3.32. Occasionally an action will have an Open command recorded that refers to a specific file. However, during batch processing you most likely want the action to run on the files being batched (those selected in the File Browser, in a specific folder, opened files in Photoshop, etc.) rather than the files specified when the action was originally recorded. If the action does contain such an Open command, checking Override Action "Open" Commands will bypass opening the file specified in the action and only perform the action on those included in the batch. An Open command must be present in the action in order for this to work properly: Batch does not automatically open the source files.

Figure 3.32 Select Override Action "Open" Commands only if there is an Open Image command in the action; otherwise, the batch will not work properly.

 Note: If the action is designed to operate on already-open files or if specific files need be called (such as Illustrator files) in order for the action to function properly, leave this unchecked.

You can avoid some dialogs by checking Suppress File Open Options Dialogs. This option can be useful regardless of whether or not any "Open" steps are recorded as part of the action; it suppresses supplemental dialogs (such as Rasterize for vector graphics) that appear during playback, specifically when those file types are selected for opening in the action. This option is also useful for batch processing Camera Raw files. By bypassing the options dialogs on these file types, the default settings, or those previously specified, will be used and the Open dialog will be skipped.

Finally, checking the Include All Subfolders or Suppress Color Profile Warnings options do just what they say. Leave the color profile warning option unchecked if you want to see them when they occur.

In the next area, you choose a destination. The Destination drop-down menu contains three items (see Figure 3.33):

None Select this item if you want to leave the images open in Photoshop.

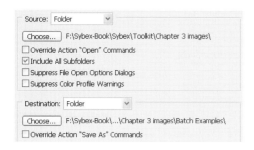

Figure 3.33 Choose a source where the images to be processed can be found, as well as a destination where they should be placed after processing is complete.

Save And Close Select this item if you want to overwrite the original images with the new version after the action has processed them. (I strongly recommend against this option: this will replace your original images, and that is rarely a good thing.) One option is to duplicate the originals to another folder in advance and then run the Batch command on the duplicate folder, ensuring your originals stay intact.

Folder Select this item if you want to choose a folder on your computer in which to save the new files. When you select this item, the Choose button becomes available; you can also create a folder where you would like the images saved from the Choose dialog box that appears when you click the Choose button.

Immediately following a destination selection is a check box similar to the one discussed earlier. Use the Override Action "Save As" Commands check box only if the action contains a Save command. When you check this box, a dialog box opens (see Figure 3.34), warning you that a Save command must be present in the action; if not, no files will be saved. Also, if you want to run a process that saves to a different file format than the original image, you must record the Save As command as part of the action. By using the Override Action "Save As" Commands option, you can tell the Batch process to save to a different folder location than the one that was recorded within the action.

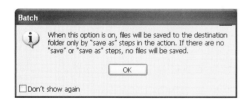

Figure 3.34 Select the Override Action "Save As" Commands check box only if a Save command is recorded into the action.

In the next area of the Batch dialog box you set up a naming convention for your new images. This can range from a single digit or letter to an extremely long name containing serial numbers, date (by month, day, and year), file extensions, and a whole jumble of numbers and letters sequentially ordered by the Batch command (see Figure 3.35). Each of the six drop-down menus lets you add serial numbers, dates, and so forth to the names of the images. Figure 3.35 also shows a list from one of these menus; each of these menus contains the same list. The important thing to remember is that you need to select an extension from the final drop-down menu. The naming convention you choose is up to you; generally I use a three-digit numbering or lettering system with a file extension when processing folders, for simplicity.

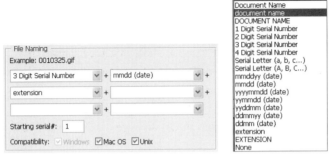

Figure 3.35 Establish a naming convention for the processed images using the six drop-down menus. Each menu has a host of options (right); ensure that the final one you use has Extension selected.

In the last area of the Batch dialog box you tell the Batch command what to do when it encounters an error. You have two options: Stop For Errors (stop the batch processing immediately until the error is cleared) or Log Errors To File. If you intend to be away from your computer during the processing, it is best to log the errors to file so that processing will continue. For instance, if an action is designed to run on RGB images but the action comes across an image in Grayscale mode, the action might stop as it will not know what to do with this other image. If this occurs 20 minutes after you leave and you expect several hundred images to be processed when you have returned to work, you will find that no additional images were processed beyond that point. If you select Log Errors To File, Photoshop saves the error message and continues processing the rest of the images.

Click the Save As button, directly below the Errors drop-down menu, to establish how and where the error log will be saved for your review later.

Once all this is set up and you click OK, the images are processed and saved, as per your direction in the Batch dialog box. This nifty tool, which can only be run with actions, can save hours and even days of processing time, which can equate to a lot of money for a production studio or a photographer.

Creating and Applying Droplets

The only real difference between the Batch command and Droplets is that a Droplet is in effect an executable file or a mini-program that can reside outside Photoshop. The dialog box in which you create a Droplet is nearly identical to that of the Batch command, as you'll see shortly.

The thing that makes Droplets cool is simply the shortcut factor. You can record a Droplet with a specific action assigned to it and place it on your Desktop or in a folder on your computer. Dragging an image file or a folder of images onto the Droplet executes Photoshop for you and processes the images automatically.

To open the Create Droplet dialog box, choose File > Automate > Create Droplet. The only real difference between the Batch and Create Droplet dialog boxes is the top portion. (See Figure 3.31, earlier in this chapter, for the Batch dialog box.) In the Create Droplet dialog box, click the Choose button to specify where to save the Droplet. Everything else is exactly the same as the Batch dialog box. By clicking Choose you can find or create a folder on your computer in which to save the Droplet, or you can simply place the Droplet on your Desktop for quick and painless application.

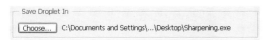

As with the Batch command, it is important to establish a separate folder for the images that are processed by the Droplet so as not to overwrite the original images. You can create the folder from the Browse For Folder dialog box that opens when you click Choose (see Figure 3.36).

Figure 3.36 The Browse For Folder dialog box

After you set up the Droplet, click OK, but this time no images will be processed. Rather you'll be asked to find a place to save the new Droplet on your hard drive. You can choose to save it to a folder, to your Desktop, or wherever you feel it would be easier for you to access (see Figure 3.37).

Figure 3.37 Find a place on your hard drive to save the Droplet

Testing and Troubleshooting Actions

Testing actions after you create them is an extremely important step. After you finish recording, run the new actions a few times on different images, image sizes, images with differing modes, and so forth. This will not only help you fine-tune the action or categorize it for specific image types, but prevent the need for troubleshooting.

When testing actions, especially those that can be used on more than one platform, do so on both Mac and PC. If you do not own both (which for most of us is probably the case), ask a friend or colleague with Photoshop installed on a different system to check it out for you. Be sure to tell them exactly what you are trying to do, what specifics about the image need to be met before starting, and what the result should be when they are done.

If you don't have anyone close with a different operating system but have access to the Internet, I recommend joining a good Photoshop forum (such as can be found at PhotoshopCafe.com) and simply asking for action testers. I do this on occasion and have had excellent responses and results: I've also made quite a few friends along the way due to mutual interest in actions.

One last point about testing: if you end up sending your action or actions out for testing and ask for a review, prepare to accept a little constructive criticism. If you ask people to give you their opinion, they will, and it may not always be the stunning praise you might expect. When I review actions, I try to be friendly, helpful, but most of all honest. Some people accept the critique in the helpful vein it is offered, but a minority take any opinion as a full frontal assault on their skills. If you ask for help, expect it; if it does turn out to be beneficial, learn from it.

Troubleshooting Actions

Although actions are great tools, errors inevitably occur. The reasons for errors are as varied and vast as the program itself; as a result there is no possible way I could show you how to correct every error in every instance. This book would become an encyclopedia rather than a quick reference. What I can do, however, is offer you a few quick checks you can perform to get your actions functioning properly.

Generally, actions that you create will not offer many problems: you will be familiar with what you were trying to do, with the disposition of the image types the action was created for, and so forth. An action actually documents your workflow: if you like to do things in a certain order, the action will reflect that pattern. So when one of your actions starts acting up, you can usually figure out what you are doing differently and either set up your image to meet the action's criteria and edit the action to process the new image type, or simply record a new action altogether.

When an action created by another party acts up, finding the problem may not be quite as intuitive. Whether your own actions or those developed by someone else give you problems, there are a few things you can try to get them running on your system.

When an error occurs, the action will stop playback to display an error message. The action will then ask you if you want to continue or stop the action (see Figure 3.38).

Figure 3.38 An action error message

To track a problem, follow these steps:

1. Stop the Action.

2. If the Actions palette is not in List mode, open the Action menu and uncheck Button mode.

3. If the error occurred after a few commands had executed, open the History palette and return the image to its original state.

4. Set the options in the Playback Options dialog box for the action (see Figure 3.39) to Step By Step or Pause For. If you select the latter, set the delay to 1 or 2 seconds.

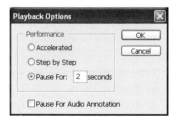

Figure 3.39 Setting a delay in the Playback Options dialog box helps track where errors occur during playback.

5. Ensure that all the check boxes toggling commands on or off are checked.

6. Hold down the Command/Control key and click the Toggle Dialog On/Off check box next to the action name to turn on all the dialog boxes on (see Figure 3.40).

Figure 3.40 Action with all Dialog Boxes turned on

7. Select the action name again in the palette so that the action will start at the beginning.

8. Play the action.

9. When the error occurs again, stop the action and review what you have seen.

    •   What did the message say?

    •   Did your image, to the best of your knowledge, meet the criteria of the action? For instance, if the action was recorded to work on an RGB image, but the photo you are attempting to run it on is indexed, you may receive an error.

    •   Did you follow all included directions exactly?

During Playback

If Stops are embedded in the action, ensure that you have met the criteria for those Stop messages. For instance, if you are running an action that requires you to enter type in the document, a common error is to use the wrong type tool. Many of my type effects actions ask the user to use the Type Mask tool. When the action asks that text be entered with the Type Mask tool but the Standard Type tool is used, an error will occur because the action will look for a selection rather than a text layer.

Often you can correct action problems by simply following the action more closely, verifying that commands are turned on, or altering settings in a dialog box. For example, if an action is trying to reduce the size of a selection, but the dialog box is set to reduce the selection to the point where there is no longer a selection, an error will occur. Changing the setting should correct the problem, allowing the action to continue normally.

Another thing to look at is the necessity of the step. Will omitting it seriously alter the action? Try toggling the step off and replaying the action on the image. I know from experience that often a step will be recorded that is unneeded to achieve the desired end result. I'm frequently guilty of it, and many of the actions I review are as well.

Finally, if an action just doesn't seem to want to cooperate no matter what you do, record the action again, making only the needed changes to conform to the image type you are working on or need the action for. Although this may seem like a last resort, actually at times it is simply easier to record another action than to fix an existing one.

Troubleshooting actions becomes more intuitive the more you know and understand the technique you are trying to perform and the greater your experience with the software. Taking care during recording, thoroughly testing, and having an eye for spotting and correcting errors during troubleshooting will help you build a photo manipulation/correction toolbox of your own that will be custom fit for your needs and the envy of your peers. With a few actions at your disposal, you can be out taking pictures while your cohorts are sitting in front of their computers wishing they could speed up the editing process.

You're Well Equipped!

You should now have enough firepower and knowledge to begin not only creating actions, but applying those actions to single or multiple files. Actions—by themselves or in conjunction with the Batch command and Droplets—give you exceptional power in automating Photoshop and reducing the amount of time to process multiple photos. This frees you to tackle other tasks related to your business or hobby while Photoshop takes over the repetitive tasks, effectively working for you even while you're away from the computer.

Keep in mind that actions (and therefore the Batch command and Droplets) are only as intelligent as the person setting them up. This is a learning process just like anything else: you will run into situations that perhaps are not mentioned in this book that you have to navigate on your own through trial and error. You'll soon find, as you work with actions, the methodology that works best for you, the naming conventions that are easiest for you to understand, and other little nuances in the software that can only be explained and hurdled by experience.

Actions can be simple, and actions can be extremely complex. I encourage you to get into the Actions palette and experiment. Start with actions created by others, and move on to recording your own. It may take some mental elbow grease, but I'm sure that once things begin to click in your mind and you get some practical time working with these cool little scripts,they will increase your productivity and decrease the amount of time spent processing images manually. You will have an extremely capable employee named Adobe Photoshop handling the repetitive tasks for you.

Other Action Tidbits

This chapter covers a few important facts about actions that you should consider. These tidbits will help you make the most of your actions, as well as provide solid reference information.

Chapter Contents

Platform and Photoshop Version Compatibility

If you intend to use actions created on other operating systems or with earlier or later versions of Photoshop, you need to consider some compatibility issues. These are also important if you intend to create actions to share with the masses or to swap between computers. Dealing with these considerations in advance will help ease the transition between systems and help avoid frustration from actions that will not work on one computer or version but that worked perfectly fine when created.

Photoshop Versions

Actions created on some versions of Photoshop may not be compatible or play correctly on other versions of Photoshop. For instance, actions created on newer versions of the software generally do not work properly or will not even load in earlier versions of the software. Actions created on older versions of the software will work in newer versions such as Adobe Photoshop CS; however, they may not work properly, and you may need to update them in the new version of the software. For this reason, if you plan to distribute your actions to others, keep in mind your target audience and which version of software they are most likely to be using. If you intend to create actions to sell to a production studio, find out beforehand which version of Photoshop they are using and which operating system they are running so that you can do your best to record actions compatible with their business requirements.

For the most part, actions created with Adobe Photoshop 6 and Adobe Photoshop 7 can run on either version. Be aware that Adobe Photoshop 7 included a few commands that did not exist in version 6; these, of course, will not work if actions recorded in version 7 are played back in Photoshop 6. You are sure to receive an error message. Occasionally Photoshop 6 will simply bypass the command you cannot find, displaying no error message. Although this may seem like a good thing, the results will most likely will not be what you expect. Keep an eye out for skipped commands when you find yourself in this situation. A quick way to verify that all the commands are being played is to simply look at the History palette and compare it with the Actions palette in List mode.

 Note: Compatibility of actions between products varies. For instance, you cannot use Photoshop actions in ImageReady, but some Photoshop actions work in Photoshop Elements 2. Also, actions in ImageReady have several features not available in Photoshop, especially the ability to build in conditional logic—for example, processing only files that exceed a certain size.

Actions created in Photoshop 5 or 5.5, as a rule, do not function properly in later versions of the software. In many cases, the actions from 5.5 or earlier will not load into the Actions palette in version 6 or later. These days you would be hard-pressed to find any 5 or 5.5 version actions available. (The Adobe Exchange website at `http://share .studio.adobe.com` does have quite a few actions created by contributors to the site.) If you do happen to get an error message in later versions of the software saying that an action set cannot be loaded, this may be the problem.

Note: When recording your actions for distribution, take the time to insert a Stop message indicating which version of the software the action was recorded on, as well as the operating system. End users will find this extremely helpful when troubleshooting problems with the action, provided it does not function properly on their system.

Operating Systems

If you plan to distribute actions, keep in mind operating system compatibility. Photoshop runs nearly identically on both Mac operating systems and Windows. The primary difference involves keyboard shortcuts. For instance, the Ctrl key used in combination with other keys is foundational to a Windows user; Photoshop has dozens of keyboard combinations that use the Ctrl key. On a Mac, however, the key is Command. If you use keyboard shortcuts while recording your actions, Photoshop will record the step as being the result of the keyboard combination. Consequently, you can get error messages when a Mac looks for a PC shortcut and vice versa. As a rule, try not to use keyboard shortcuts when recording actions if they can be used on other platforms.

Additional Action Tips

Here are a few additional tips for recording actions that will benefit you and those who use your scripts.

- Try to keep the number of displayed dialog boxes and Stop messages to a minimum. Your actions will feel more streamlined the fewer times the action must stop to display a message or ask for user input. You can always alter the settings of a command (as discussed in Chapter 2) and receive the action with the new settings under a different name. The point is to have a clean action that helps automate repetitive tasks or perform multiple functions with minimal user input. If the action stops after every few steps to display a message or ask for input on a command setting, it becomes more of a distraction than a benefit. Trust me on this one.

- Establish a color-coding system for your actions so that when the palette is in Button mode you will be able to easily recognize, simply by the color, whether the action is for image adjustment, a command shortcut, a special effect, or a filter application. Set a standard and then stick with it.

- When naming your actions and action sets, try to use short, descriptive, relevant names or even use a coded lettering system to categorize your actions and keep track of them. This in conjunction with a color-coding system will help you find actions easily, and that in turn will help you further shorten the amount of time it takes to perform a task or function. Actions save time, and having a solid organization system for your actions saves even more time.

- Use the keyboard shortcuts available to you. Photoshop allows for 60 key combinations to be attached to actions. If you have several hundred actions, you can still use the 60 combinations; however, try not to have more than one action with a particular key combination loaded at one time.

- Save, save, save! In other words, save your actions frequently. If you alter an action, do not save the file under the same name; change the name and save the action set as a new file. You'll find your Toolbox quickly building, with multiple actions that perform variations in the same vein. Saving actions in the middle of a process is fine also, and recommended. You can always start recording again, and this is much better than losing the previous steps altogether as can happen if the computer suddenly reboots, the power surges, and so on.

- If you include a Save As command in an action that saves the file as a JPEG, ensure that the Save As Copy check box is checked in the Save As dialog box. If not, the action will open the Save As dialog box every time the action is run. When you save a copy of the JPEG, Photoshop recognizes your initial parameters and ignores the dialog box when that command opens during playback. In this way you also retain the original image and have a copy in a new folder. Retaining the original is always a good thing; overwriting the original is usually a heartbreaking experience.

Using Actions as Learning Tools

This is one of my favorite tricks, as you can probably tell if you've read anything I've written before. I include the step in most of my books simply because, when I was starting out in Photoshop, this single tip helped me more in learning the program than any book, tutorial, or other teaching resource. My frequent collaborator, Colin Smith, has made this a point of friendly ridicule, as he knows my work and also knows that I include this tip in nearly all my writing. Hey, if it works, why fix it?

An action, at its most basic, is a text file. Photoshop assigns a .atn file extension to the text document so that Photoshop can recognize this text file as an action that can be loaded and played in the software. By reading or printing this text directly, you can manually re-create the cool things performed by actions recorded by other people. Every command and every setting for those commands is listed for you so you can duplicate the steps at your leisure and learn from them.

To save an action or a set of actions as a text file, you must take one important step first. Ensure that only the action set that you want to save as a text file is loaded into Photoshop, with no others resident in that Actions palette. If you do not remove the other actions or action sets, every command from every action in the palette is saved in the text document. If you have many actions or even a few actions with many commands, your text document may turn out to be 60 to 100 to who knows how many pages long.

Here's the process for saving an action set as a text file.

1. Load only the action set that you want a text file copy of loaded into the Actions palette. Figure 4.1 shows the Actions palette with one action set containing two actions loaded. The commands are expanded so you can see the settings. As long as the actions are saved to your hard drive (or external drive), it is fine to clear the palette. Ensure that they are saved and clear them, and you can always load them again.

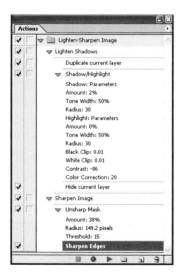

Figure 4.1 The Actions palette with two expanded actions

2. Select the action set name; otherwise, the Save Actions option will not be available.

3. While holding down the Ctrl+Alt keys (Windows) or Command+Option keys (Mac), open the Actions menu and choose Save Actions.

4. The Save dialog box opens. Note that, rather than giving the option to save with the .atn extension, the format is listed as Actions (*.TXT). Name and save the new text file to a folder on your hard drive (see Figure 4.2).

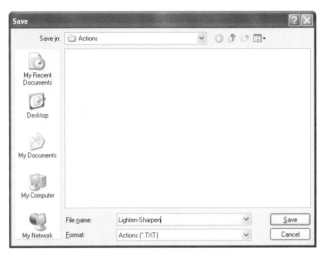

Figure 4.2 Saving the actions as a single text file

Now you can use Notepad, Word, TextEdit, or another text program to open the action and view every step and command setting for each action in that set (see Figure 4.3).

Figure 4.3 An action text file viewed in Notepad. All commands and settings for those commands are listed sequentially for each action.

If you find this helpful, I suggest you create a binder for your Photoshop action tutorials. This is especially helpful when you find an action created by another person and you want to know the secret of how they did it. With this trick, Photoshop is not good at keeping secrets!

Actions and Camera Raw Files

As cameras become more sophisticated and the prices drop, more photographers can work with camera raw files rather than images reduced in size by the camera itself. Photoshop comes with its own dialog box for these files, and creating actions for them takes some thought. Here's the process.

To open camera raw images with an action, follow these steps:

1. Create a new action. (Be sure to choose or create the set first.) Name the action—something like "My Camera Raw Action" will do just fine—and click Record.

2. Open the camera raw file and record the commands/steps you want as you would with any other action.

3. Adobe recommends you record the action with Selected Image chosen in the Settings menu of the Camera Raw dialog box. This way each image's particular settings from either the Camera Raw database or XMP sidecar files will be used when replaying the action.

4. Stop recording and save the action set.

Note: When you use an action to open camera raw images, the Camera Raw plug-in settings are based on those that were in place when the action was recorded. If you have camera raw files with specific settings, you might want to record a new action specific to the file.

The Batch command can open camera raw files directly from a digital camera. To do this, be sure the camera is plugged into your computer when setting up the batch, and select Import as the source. The camera should appear (provided it is turned on and you have already set up your computer to recognize the connection).

Online Resources for Actions

Here are some prime places where you can download Photoshop actions, often for free (and many created by me):

Action Fx Photoshop Resources (http://actionfx.com) This is my website. I started it a few years ago as a hobby dedicated to actions; it has expanded drastically to include tutorials, layer styles, brushes, and other resources made especially for Photoshop enthusiasts like me. A large free area and a *huge* member's area. Come check it out!

Adobe Studio Exchange (`http://share.studio.adobe.com`) Adobe's answer for the actions enthusiast. This site is packed with actions, as well as all manner of files for all manner of Adobe products that you can download here. You are encouraged to share your work with the masses, as you may upload your own creations. This website is an excellent resource for building your Photoshop arsenal.

PhotoshopUser.com: The Official NAPP Members Website (`www.photoshopuser.com`) OK, I admit it. I created most of the actions you find on the official National Association of Photoshop Professionals (NAPP) website. I am the official NAPP actions guru, after all. This site is available only to members of NAPP; if you are not one already, I encourage you to join. A subscription to *Photoshop User* magazine is included, and that alone is worth the price of membership. I also write for this site, so be sure to check out the tutorials!

Photoshop Café (`www.photoshopcafe.com`) This is award-winning Photoshop guru Colin Smith's site. Colin and I collaborate frequently, and he has a few of my actions available for download. Stop in and say hello on the forum… I'm usually lurking there somewhere.

HTML Center (`www.htmlcenter.com`) Some of my older actions are available for download on this excellent resource website. Most of these were created with Photoshop 6 or earlier, so they may not work on Photoshop CS. Still, it's worth a shot!

Fred Miranda (`www.fredmiranda.com/`; click the Software button for Photoshop actions) This is a professional website with the professional photographer or Photoshop user in mind.

Finally, here are even more online locations where you can obtain ready-to-use actions:

www.shutterfreaks.com/Actions/Actions.html

www.teamphotoshop.com/

www.photoshoproadmap.com/

www.redscreen.net/

www.photoshop-stuff.com

http://adactio.com/

http://graphicssoft.about.com/cs/photoshopactiontip/

www.gormly.com/ericsfx/

www.outdooreyes.com/photosection20.php3

www.bytephoto.com/

www.timo2000.de/

Guide to the Toolkit CD

The companion CD to this book is organized to make navigation and use easy. This guide reflects the sorting system on the CD, lists all the contents, and explains and demonstrates a few key actions in each category.

The CD is organized into the following sections:

Photography These are my own actions dealing with continuous-tone photographic images. These actions are gathered into five categories: Aging, Artistic, Color Correction, Enhancement, and Layout.

Production These actions help you manage Photoshop itself. With them you can manipulate layers, settings within the software, and a variety of menial tasks to aid you in saving time while working.

Typography These are my actions for creating custom, stylish type effects. This is just a small sample of the vast number of such actions I have created; if you enjoy these, please visit my website (http://actionfx.com) for more.

Additional Plug-Ins and Add-ons This section includes additional goodies I created that you can plug right into Photoshop and use to help explore your artistic talents and enhance your work: layer styles, custom brushes, patterns, and custom shapes.

Third-Party Actions, Add-Ons, and Stock Images Here you'll find actions that have been contributed by some of the best Photoshop developers. Images referenced in the text and used in the walk-through portions of the book are also provided here, plus tutorials, demos, and other teaching tools.

Actions from the Book

The text refers to several actions. To aid you in finding these actions, their locations are given here:

AFX-CloudsOverWaterCS.atn	Type Actions folder
AFX-OiledMetalCS-1.atn	Type Actions folder
AFX-PencilSketch.atn	Included in the AFX-SketchesCS-01 action set, Photo-Artistic folder
AFX-SketchesCS-1.atn	Photo-Artistic folder
PTK-Image_Sharpening.atn	Photo-Enhancement folder

Photo: Aging

Almost an artistic style of its own, the process of aging photos is very popular. Photoshop actions can provide multiple variations of the technique, from simple sepia to advanced wear and tear.

Sample Aging Action

PhotoAging-02

This action (included in the PTK-PhotoAgingCS-01 action set) offers one variation of aging, including streaks and enhanced grain.

The Ultimate

Photoshop Actions

Color Gallery

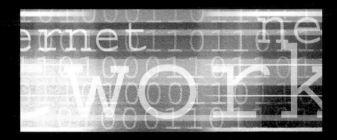

This book has talked about how actions can help you automate processes in Photoshop, but I'm not stopping there. The CD is packed with actions for you to use as they are, to edit for your own use, and to learn from. This section gives examples of some of the dynamic corrections and alterations available to you with the included software.

Actions can help you create stylized moods for your photos. **LEFT**: original; **RIGHT**: after the PTK-Age-Contrast-Portrait action.

Use actions to add age and texture. **TOP**: original; **BOTTOM**: after the PhotoAging-01 action.

Actions make painting and sketching multiple images a breeze. **TOP**: original; **BOTTOM**: after the Paint-Sketch-02 action.

Bitmap effects are easily achieved. **TOP**: original; **BOTTOM**: after the Photo-to-Clipart04 action.

Color and lighting adjustments done automatically, enhancing those special moments. **LEFT**: original; **RIGHT**: after the LightenShadowsCS-01 action.

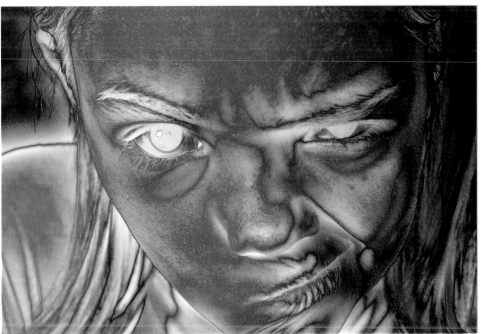

Alter color in your images for stark, sometimes shocking, results. **TOP**: original; **BOTTOM**: after the Grungy-Color action.

Dark Gothic creations are a snap. **TOP**: original; **BOTTOM**: after the SelectionArt-01 action.

Turn your photo collections into comic style art. **TOP**: original; **BOTTOM**: after the PhotoToComic-01 action.

Turn photos to pencil sketches without getting your hands dirty. **TOP**: original; **BOTTOM**: after the PencilSketch-01 action.

Turn scenes and people over onto themselves, creating stunning landscapes and strange creatures. **LEFT**: original; **RIGHT**: after the Simple-Mirror action.

Format your art for use on CD labels to stylize your music and video collections. **TOP**: original; **BOTTOM**: after the AFX-CD-Label action.

Photos with nasty color casts can be quickly restored with natural tones. **LEFT**: original; **RIGHT**: after the Correct-YellowGreen-Cast action.

Newspaper prints are another variation on line art. **TOP**: original; **BOTTOM**: after the Newspaper-Sketch action.

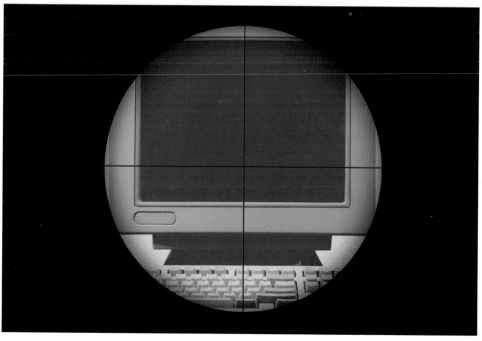

Target your subjects or product quickly and painlessly. **TOP**: original; **BOTTOM**: after the Bullseye-Nightshot action.

Actions can help you adjust your preferences. In this case, the gray transparency squares have been removed, though the background remains transparent. **LEFT**: original; **RIGHT**: after the TransparencyGrid-Off action.

Quickly add borders, frames, and drop shadows. **TOP**: original; **BOTTOM**: after the Sharp-Drop-Shadow01 action.

Poor digital shots can be corrected with just a few steps. **TOP**: original; **BOTTOM**: after the Model-Shot01 action.

Merge images to create stylish or eerie artistic renderings. **TOP**: original; **BOTTOM**: after the Photo-Merge01 action.

Soften areas while focusing on others. **TOP**: original; **BOTTOM**: after the Sharp-to-Blur01 action.

Increase the quality of your black-and-white shots. **LEFT**: original; **RIGHT**: after the Better Grayscale action.

Image dissections and frames provide interesting new ways to display your photos. **TOP**: original; **BOTTOM**: after the Screens action.

The Polaroid Frame is a popular effect and is easily achieved with an action. **TOP**: original; **BOTTOM**: after the Polaroid-300ppi action.

Actions are excellent tools for converting the modes of individual or multiple images, as well as assigning color for print. Select from multiple actions in the Mode Conversion Actions.atn set that convert to duotone, tritone, and quadtone, or edit these actions to suit your own requirements. **LEFT**: original; **RIGHT**: after the conversion.

Adding or changing commands is easy. The examples here (from wildStripes in Chapter 2) are basically from the same action, with just a few commands added to generate the second result.

Combining filters in actions offers quality art for prints. **LEFT**: original; **RIGHT**: after the Photo-to-Sketch-01 action.

Turn your photos into seamless patterns. **TOP**: original;
BOTTOM: after the Photo-to-Seamless02 action.

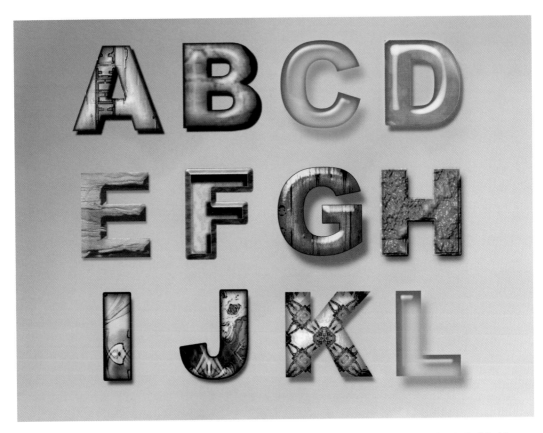

The CD also contains layer styles (several demonstrated here) that you can apply to your frames, text, or buttons with a single click of the mouse. Gels, glass, wood, stone, and metal effects are just a click away.

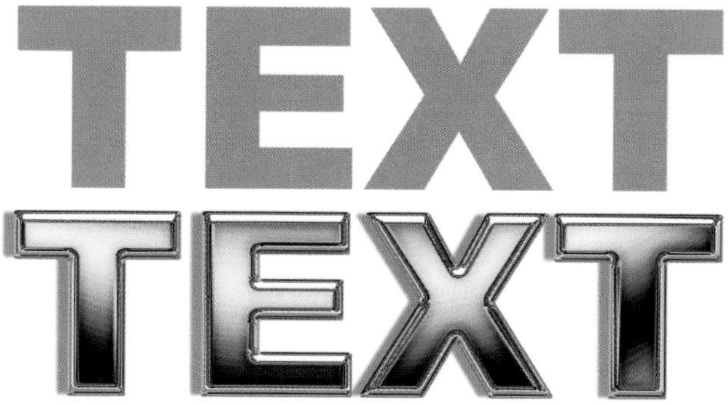

TEXT

TEXT

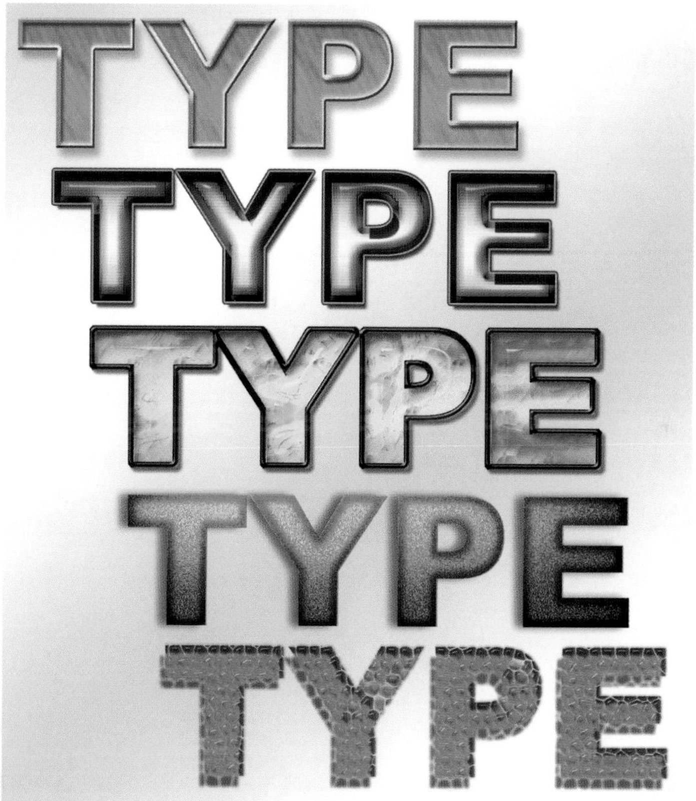

TYPE

TYPE

TYPE

TYPE

TYPE

TOP: Photo adjustments aren't the only things you can automate: text effects from scratch are extremely popular and are easily "actionable." In this shot, the gray type above was converted to steel with one click of the Action Start button, using the AFX-MetalMasterCS-01 action. **BOTTOM**: Still more variations of typography actions. (This image used a variety of actions from the PTK-TYPE-CS-Set01 action set.) These actions aren't restricted to text: they can be applied to shapes and selections of all types. These are great for building themed website buttons or image frames as well.

Even people can be transformed into a background, pattern, or texture: different photos offer stunning variations, all from the same action. **TOP**: original; **BOTTOM**: after the Photo-to-Seamless01 action.

Apply patterns to your photos for stylish effects. This action (find it in the PTK-Additional Layer Actions.atn action set) will create a pattern-filled adjustment layer. **TOP:** original; **BOTTOM:** adding a pattern and changing the blending mode gives a decidedly dynamic rendering of the original photo.

Give your models the attention they deserve. **LEFT**: original; **RIGHT**: after the Model-Spotlight-Warming action.

All Aging Actions

Set: *PTK-PhotoAgingCS-01.atn*

The only action set in the Aging category is PTK-PhotoAgingCS-01, which contains these actions:

- PTK-Age-Contrast-Portrait
- PhotoAging-01
- PhotoAging-02 (example above)
- PhotoAging-03: Harsh aging, streaks, and blemishes.
- PhotoAging-04: This action offers a subtle sepia-style effect, with a lined texture foundation.
- PhotoAging-05: Similar to the previous action, with a greater degree of fading.
- PhotoAging-06: Uses difference clouds to blemish the photo. Produces very harsh aging.
- PhotoAging-07: Sepia style, with vertical streaks/water paper foundation.
- Aged-Print-01
- Aged-Print-02: Similar to the Photo-Aging actions, with more natural color retained. Harsh white areas.
- Aged-Print-03: Makes the photo appear grainy, with light and dark blemishes. Also has spots of wear, making the photo appear to have suffered physical damage.
- Stained-with-Age: More of a black-and-white photo effect with streaks and areas of light and dark blemishing.
- Scratches-and-Blemishes: As the name states. Overall effect is a two-toned scratched and blemished photo. This is a personal favorite of mine.

Photo: Artistic

This is my favorite group of the bunch. In these actions, I've put together some of my favorite artistic effects for photos. Convert your images to line art, to oil paintings, and even to seamless patterns that resemble nothing like the original image. I've even included a few experiments that you can work with.

Sample Artistic Actions

Photo-to-Clipart01

One of four clip art actions, this process (illustrated in the Color Section) uses the Threshold filter to generate a colored, grainy, and seemingly painted rendering of your photograph. This action (included in the PTK-PhotoArtSet-A action set) has a short runtime and can produce interesting results on different types of photos.

PencilSketch-01

Something I wish that I had the ability to do is to sit down and draw. Although I've never had the talent to sketch anything more complicated than a doodle, Photoshop has a variety of tools that you can use to make realistic sketches. This action (included in the PTK-PhotoArtSet-A action set) renders a high-detail sketch of the subject photo. In the example, take a look at the detail in the ringlets in the model's hair.

Photo-on-Canvas

As in PTK-PhotoArtSet-A, this action continues with more artistic ways in which to convert your photos into artist renderings. For example, the Photo-on-Canvas action (in PTK-PhotoArtSet-B) gives the impression that the photo has been transferred to a canvas or other cloth material.

WallPaint-PhotoGraffiti

If I'm clumsy with a pencil, I'm even worse with a paintbrush or a can of spray paint. This action (included in the PTK-PhotoArtSet-B action set) takes care of that problem, by turning your photos into murals on the side of a brick wall.

Ribbons-02

I realize that I'm showing a lot of examples from this group of actions, but it really is my favorite bunch. With the Ribbons-02 action (and two other variations, all in the PTK-PhotoArtSet-B action set), break out your digital scissors and start cutting! These actions are great for people who get angry easily, but don't want to damage anything in the "real" world.

Grungy-3_Tone

This action is in the PTK-PhotoEffects-01 action set. It is actually a combination of effects (aging, colorizing) that create an interesting drawn/contrast appearance. This action also puts a Gradient Map adjustment layer to good use.

Imposed-in-Copper

This action uses the Photoshop filters, Bas Relief in particular, to "etch" your photo into a copper-toned backdrop. The end effect gives the appearance of a raised image in metal or a stonelike substance. This action is in the PTK-Photo Experiment.atn action set.

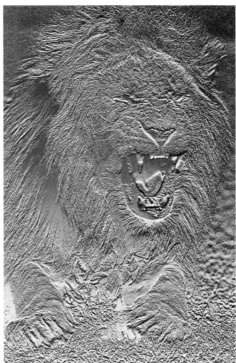

AFX-Pattern Creator 23

In all, I have included 50 pattern-generating actions for your use. If you have a lot of images just taking up space on your hard drive, try running these actions on them for some rather startling results. You can use the patterns that are produced for a number of things: backdrops and patterns for layer styles are just a couple. The image shown here is from AFX-Patter Creator 23, in the `PTK-Pattern Actions.atn` action set.

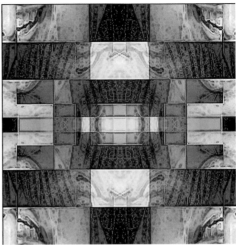

AFX-Pattern Creator 32

This image shows another example of the intense results you can get from this pattern set. This image was created by AFX-Patter Creator 32, in the `PTK-Pattern Actions.atn` action set.

All Artistic Actions

Set: *PTK-PhotoArtSet-A.atn*

- Photo-to-Clipart01 (an example is in the Color Section)
- Photo-to-Clipart02: Harsh separation of light and dark areas to black and white.
- Photo-to-Clipart03: Not really a clip-art effect; this is more a black and white with grain.
- Photo-to-Clipart04: Makes your photo look like a pixelated bitmap consisting of black and white dots (as you might find on a printed page).
- ContrastPaint-01
- Paint-Sketch-01 (example earlier in this guide)
- Paint-Sketch-02: Colored pencil drawing effect.
- Paint-Sketch-03: More a photo and paint combination. Textured.
- Paint-Sketch-04: Soft subject, lightly textured.
- Paint-Sketch-05
- Paint-Sketch-06
- Paint-Sketch-07
- Paint-Sketch-08
- Photo-to-Sketch-01
- PhotoToComic-01 (an example is in the Color Section)
- PhotoToComic-02
- PencilSketch-01
- Newspaper-Sketch: Turns photo into a pixelated, newspaper-style print.

Set: *PTK-PhotoArtSet-B.atn*

- Canvas_Painting
- Colored_Pencil01
- Colored_Pencil02
- SelectionArt-01
- Photo-on-Canvas (example earlier in this guide)
- Photo-on-Canvas02
- Texture Sketch
- Black-SubtleColorPaint
- Ribbons-01
- Ribbons-02 (example earlier in this guide)

- Ribbons-03
- AddGrain
- WallPaint-PhotoGraffiti (example earlier in this guide)
- BlueArt
- Fire-Reflection
- Fire-Reflection_02
- Blue-Reflection

Set: *PTK-PhotoEffects-01.atn*

- Simple-Mirror: Reflects the left side of the photo onto the right.
- Simple-Mirror02: Reflects the right side of the photo onto the left.
- Simple-Mirror03: Slight variation on Simple-Mirror02.
- Simple-Mirror04: Slight variation on Simple-Mirror.
- Grungy-BW
- Grungy-BW02: Uses a gradient map to separate the lights and darks, giving the image a metallic feel.
- Grungy-Color: Combines photo with painterly elements.
- Grungy-3_Tone (example earlier in this guide)

Set: *PTK-Photo Experiments.atn*

- Bullseye-Nightshot
- Photo-Merge01
- Imposed-in-Copper (example earlier in this guide)
- ExtremePixilation

Set: *PTK-Pattern Actions.atn*

The actions in this set turn a standard photo into something quite different. Most of the end effects are seamless, leaving you with plenty of material to use as backgrounds or to save as patterns for use with layer styles.

- AFX-Pattern Creation 1
- AFX-Pattern Creation 2
- AFX-Pattern Creation 3
- AFX-Pattern Creation 4
- AFX-Pattern Creation 5
- AFX-Pattern Creation 6

- AFX-Pattern Creation 7
- AFX-Pattern Creation 8
- AFX-Pattern Creation 9
- AFX-Pattern Creation 10
- AFX-Pattern Creation 11
- AFX-Pattern Creation 12
- AFX-Pattern Creation 13
- AFX-Pattern Creation 14
- AFX-Pattern Creation 15
- AFX-Pattern Creation 16
- AFX-Pattern Creation 17
- AFX-Pattern Creation 18
- AFX-Pattern Creation 19
- AFX-Pattern Creation 20
- AFX-Pattern Creation 21
- AFX-Pattern Creation 22
- AFX-Pattern Creation 23 (example earlier in this guide)
- AFX-Pattern Creation 24
- AFX-Pattern Creation 25
- AFX-Pattern Creation 26
- AFX-Pattern Creation 27
- AFX-Pattern Creation 28
- AFX-Pattern Creation 29
- AFX-Pattern Creation 30
- AFX-Pattern Creation 31
- AFX-Pattern Creation 32 (example earlier in this guide)
- AFX-Pattern Creation 33
- AFX-Pattern Creation 34
- AFX-Pattern Creation 35
- AFX-Pattern Creation 36
- AFX-Pattern Creation 37
- AFX-Pattern Creation 38
- AFX-Pattern Creation 39

- AFX-Pattern Creation 40
- AFX-Pattern Creation 41
- AFX-Pattern Creation 42
- AFX-Pattern Creation 43
- AFX-Pattern Creation 44
- AFX-Pattern Creation 45
- AFX-Pattern Creation 46
- AFX-Pattern Creation 47
- AFX-Pattern Creation 48
- AFX-Pattern Creation 49
- AFX-Pattern Creation 50

Set: *PTK-Pattern_Generation02.atn*

- Photo-to-Seamless01 (an example is in the Color Section)
- Photo-to-Seamless02
- Photo-to-Seamless03
- Photo-to-Seamless04

Photo: Color Correction

Adjusting, correcting, and removing color in photos is one chore that actions can help with. This section contains actions that help manage the color in your image, as well as the light/dark separations brought about by shadows and light sources.

Sample Color Correction Actions

CurvesCorrection-RGB

This action (in the DigitalPhotoCorrection action set) helps you set up curves to correct color casts inherent in digital photographs. With this action, you can change preferences for highlights, midtones, and shadows in the Curves dialog box and then continue correcting the photo with the new settings in place. To do so, follow these steps:

1. Open your image.

2. During playback, the action will ask you to sample the darkest portion of the image and also the brightest. Use the Levels eyedropper tools to do this.

3. To ensure you have sampled the darkest and lightest areas of the image, use Threshold to see those points.

   Dark images will appear lighter, and light images, darker. Simple as that!

ColorEnhance-03

Although this set of tools consists of many simple one- or two-step adjustments, Color-Enhance-03 (from the PTK-ToningTools action set) works in multiple steps to help you get the most color from your image. Simply load the action and play it on your photo; no special requirements need be met.

All Color Correction Actions

Set: *ColorSpaceForPhotos.atn*

- ChangeColorSpace-AdobeRGB1998: This action is designed to set Photoshop's color space for working with photographs.

Set: *DigitalPhotoCorrection.atn*

- SetShadow_Highlight_Midtone_RGB
- CurvesCorrection-RGB (example earlier in this guide)
- SetShadow_Highlight_Midtone_CMYK

Set: *PTK-ToningTools.atn*

- ColorEnhance-01: One of four actions that adjust/enhance/enrich the colors in your photo.
- ColorEnhance-02: Equalizes the highlights and shadows and enhances the colors of both.
- ColorEnhance-03: Brightens and sharpens the photo, as well as enhances the colors in the photo (example earlier in this guide).
- ColorEnhance-04: A sharper version than the previous actions in this group.
- LightenShadows-01
- LightenShadows-02
- ColorBalance_AddRed
- ColorBalance_AddGreen
- ColorBalance_AddBlue
- ColorBalance-LessRed-MoreCyan
- ColorBalance-LessGreen-MoreMagenta
- ColorBalance-LessBlue-MoreYellow
- ColorCorrection-Levels
- SetMidtoneGray-Levels
- Curves-DecreaseHighlights
- Curves-IncreaseHighlights
- Curves-DecreaseMidtones
- Curves-IncreaseMidtones
- Curves-IncreaseShadows
- Curves-DecreaseShadows
- Curves-Layer-IncreaseHighlights

- Curves-Layer-DecreaseHighlights
- Curves-Layer-IncreaseMidtones
- Curves-Layer-DecreaseHighlights
- Curves-Layer-IncreaseShadow
- Curves-Layer-DecreaseShadow
- Apply_Shadow-Highlight
- IncreaseContrast-Layer
- DecreaseContrast-Layer
- IncreaseSaturation-Layer
- DecreaseSaturation-Layer
- Correct-YellowGreen-Cast
- Add Blue-01
- Add Green-01
- Add Red-01
- ColorCorrection-8 Bit
- ColorCorrection-16 Bit

Photo: Enhancement

Photoshop offers expert tools for those in the know to subtly or drastically embellish photographs to get the most out of pixels. This category of actions will help you get better grayscale, sharpen photos to reveal stark details that may not have been visible originally to the naked eye, and even convert photos of family members to soft model shots.

Sample Enhancement Actions

Sharpening-07

This action (from the PTK-Image_Sharpening action set) uses the High Pass filter sharpening method to great effect.

BrightenHighlights

This action takes a slightly different approach to adjusting the brightness of an image. Considered by some a more advanced technique, it separates the highlights from a photo and places them in their own layer, separating the corrections to the highlights from the rest of the image. Although this technique (from the PTK-Photo-Adjustments set) may seem difficult if you are new to the software, this action takes care of the heavy lifting for you.

PoorReception

Actions and tutorials on creating scan lines have been around for years; this action (in the PTK-PhotoEnhance action set) is a variation on that theme. It produces an image that gives the appearance of poor television reception.

Model-Spotlight-Warming

Dress up a personal photo or those from photo shoots with this stylish action. Model-Spotlight-Warming, included in the PTK-PhotoEnhance action set, works to subdue the background, blurring it and darkening it softly while enhancing the subject of focus. You can also control the final effect, as the action prompts you to manipulate a mask to soften or increase it.

All Enhancement Actions

Set: *PTK-Image_Sharpening.atn*

You can use a variety of techniques to sharpen images in Photoshop. This set covers a few of these techniques, including variations on High Pass filter sharpening and Unsharp Mask. These actions vary in degrees of sharpening.

- Sharpening-01
- Sharpening-02
- Sharpening-03
- Sharpening-04
- Sharpening-05
- Sharpening-06
- Sharpening-07 (example earlier in this guide)
- Sharpening-08
- Sharpening-09
- Sharpening-10
- Sharpening-11
- Lab Sharpen-01
- Lab Sharpen-02

Set: *PTK-Photo-Adjustments.atn*

- Curves-LightenShadow
- Curves-BrightenHighlights
- BrightenHighlights (example earlier in this guide)
- BrightenShadows
- DarkenShadow
- Lev-Shad_Highli-Color_ADJ01
- AutoColor-AutoLevels
- AutoLevels
- Levels_Adjustment_Layer_Insert
- Color_Fill-Brighten01
- Gradient_Fill_Layer01
- Gradient_Fill_Layer02

Set: *PTK-PhotoEnhance.atn*

- Brighten-Soften-01
- Brighten-Soften02
- Model-Shot01
- Model-Shot02
- ModelShot-Sepia
- LightenShadowsCS-01
- NoiseReduce-Soften
- Sharp-to-Blur01
- Reduce Grain01
- Better Grayscale
- Better Grayscale-Dot Gain 10 Percent
- Better Grayscale-Dot Gain 15 Percent
- Better Grayscale-Dot Gain 20 Percent
- Better Grayscale-Dot Gain 25 Percent
- Better Grayscale-Dot Gain 30 Percent
- Model-Spotlight-BlueTint
- Model-Spotlight-Warming (example earlier in this guide)
- Model-Soften-SlightSepia
- PoorReception (example earlier in this guide)
- Apply_Image-RedChan-40perVivLGT
- Apply_Image-GRNChan-40perVivLGT
- Apply_Image-Bl Apply_Image-Cyan-40perVivLGTuChan-40perVivLGT
- Apply_Image-MagChan-40perVivLGT
- Apply_Image-YelChan-40perVivLGT
- Apply_Image-BLKChan-20perVivLGT

Photo: Layout

So you have all these great images you have corrected, edited, and otherwise altered. Now what do you do? This section provides you with many actions that give options for displaying your images. With these, you can apply a layout for contact sheets, create picture packages, or even turn your photo into a label for a CD. This set also contains several actions for resizing your images for different uses.

Sample Layout Actions

Contact Sheet-8x10- 3 Col_4 Row

With the Contact Sheet actions (in the action set PTK-Contact Sheets.atn), I take an automated process and streamline it. These actions take active images in the File Browser and quickly generate contact sheets, which you can easily customize.

Drop-Shadow05

Actions can help you apply quick drop shadows and other style effects to your images. The action set `PTK-Border-Shadow_Actions.atn` offers a few variations for your use.

PTK-Crop_Marks03

This action and two variations, all found in the `PTK-Crop_Marks.atn` action set, insert crop marks on the corners of your images when they are ready to head to production.

7-Photo_Layout01

You may find this hard to believe, but I've been asked many times why Photoshop doesn't let you create picture packages that people can then print and distribute. Granted, this reaction is primarily from home users. The usual reaction, when I show them that Picture Package 2 resides right in the software, is shock followed by joy followed by confusion. Check out `PTK-Picture Package-10x16_Sheet.atn`, `PTK-Picture Package-11x17_Sheet.atn`, and `PTK-Picture Packages-8x10_Sheet.atn`. These actions take away the confusion of manipulating the Picture Package 2 plug-in, automating the process so you don't have to do so.

All Layout Actions

Set: *PTK-Border-Shadow_Actions.atn*

- Sharp-Drop-Shadow01
- Drop-Shadow02
- Drop-Shadow03
- Drop-Shadow04
- Drop-Shadow05 (shown earlier in this guide)
- Drop-Shadow06

- Drop-Shadow07
- Inner-Shadow01

Set: *PTK-Contact Sheets.atn*

- Contact Sheet-8x10- 1 Col_2 Row
- Contact Sheet-8x10- 2 Col_2 Row
- Contact Sheet-8x10- 2 Col_3 Row
- Contact Sheet-8x10- 2 Col_4 Row (shown earlier in this guide)
- Contact Sheet-8x10- 3 Col_3 Row
- Contact Sheet-8x10- 3 Col_4 Row
- Contact Sheet-8x10- 3 Col_5 Row
- Contact Sheet-8x10- 4 Col_5 Row
- Contact Sheet-7x9- 1 Col_2 Row
- Contact Sheet-7x9- 2 Col_2 Row

Set: *PTK-AFX-CD-Label.atn*

- AFX-CD-Label (an example of this action is in the Color Section)

Set: *PTK-Contact Sheets-CD Case.atn*

You can use these actions to format groups of images for use on a CD cover. Start creating a library of discs with custom cases showing which images are on each.

- 4_Across-4_Down copy
- 5_Across-6_Down
- 6_Across-7_Down copy

Set: *PTK-Crop_Marks.atn*

- PTK-Crop_Marks (shown earlier in this guide)
- PTK-Crop_Marks02
- PTK-Crop_Marks03

Set: *PTK-Picture Package-10x16_Sheet.atn*

- 1-Photo_Layout01
- 2-Photo_Layout01
- 3-Photo_Layout01
- 5-Photo_Layout01

Set: *PTK-Picture Package-11x17_Sheet.atn*

- 16-Photo_Layout01

Set: *PTK-Picture Packages-8x10_Sheet.atn*

- 2-Photo_Layout01
- 3-Photo_Layout01
- 4-Photo_Layout01
- 4-Photo_Layout02
- 5-Photo_Layout01
- 6-PhotoLayout01
- 7-Photo_Layout01 (shown earlier in this guide)
- 7-Photo_Layout02
- 8-Photo_Layout01
- 8-Photo_Layout02
- 9-Photo_Layout01
- 9-Photo_Layout02
- 10-Photo_Layout01
- 12-Photo_Layout01
- 16-Photo_Layout01
- 20-Photo_Layout01

Set: *PTK-Polaroid-300ppi-01.atn*

- Polaroid-300ppi (an example is in the Color Section)

Set: *PTK-Resize Actions.atn*

This group of actions helps you resize your images. I've stepped them in percentages to help you achieve the size you require with minimal input.

- Resize-200 Percent
- Resize-150 Percent
- Resize-90 Percent
- Resize-80 Percent
- Resize-75 Percent
- Resize-50 Percent
- Resize-25 Percent
- Resize-10 Percent
- Resize-5 Percent

Set: *PTK-Screens.atn*

- Screens (an example is in the Color Section)

Production

These actions are designed to streamline the production process. With these actions you can quickly change image modes, manipulate layers, and quickly apply processes that normally require accessing those tedious menus.

Sample Production Actions

Grayscale-to-Bitmap_HalftoneScreen

This action (from the `Mode Conversion Actions.atn` action set) allows you to quickly convert a grayscale image to bitmap using the Halftone Screen method.

PosterizeAdjustmentLayer-4Levels

You can apply posterization to separate colors into varying levels, without damaging the photo. Posterizing is also great for creating art pieces that appear drawn; check out the Artistic actions to see this put to use to create comic book–style images. The example shown here demonstrates the PosterizeAdjustmentLayer-4Levels action from the `PTK-AdjustmentLayers.atn` action set.

Exact Center

This action (in the `PTK-Align_Layer_Group.atn` action set) allows you to move a text layer or any layer, for that matter, so that it is oriented in the exact center of the document.

In a multilayered document, select the layer you want to place in the center of the document, and then play the action. That's it. The action has taken care of all the centering functions for you. This works great for placing watermarks across your image.

Transform Path-Scale

Using this action, you can easily increase, decrease, or transform the size and shape of your paths. In the example, I created a path from a type layer and then increased the scale of the path using the Transform Path-Scale action from the `PTK-Path Tools.atn` set.

1. With a path active, play the action.
2. You will be asked to enter/alter the scale of the path. When the transform command pops up, simply move the corners until the path takes on the size you require.
3. Accept the change, and complete the action.

All Production Actions

Set: *Mode Conversion Actions.atn*

- Convert-to-Grayscale
- Grayscale-to-Bitmap_50-PercentThreshold
- Grayscale-to-Bitmap_PatternDither
- Grayscale-to-Bitmap_HalftoneScreen (example earlier in this guide)
- Grayscale-to-Bitmap_DiffusionDither
- Grayscale-to-Bitmap_CustomPattern
- Grayscale-to-Duotone-01

- Grayscale-to-Duotone-02
- Grayscale-to-Duotone-03
- Grayscale-to-Duotone-04
- Grayscale-to-Duotone-05
- Grayscale-to-Duotone-06
- Grayscale-to-Duotone-07
- Grayscale-to-Duotone-08
- Grayscale-to-Duotone-09
- Grayscale-to-Duotone-10
- Grayscale-to-Duotone-11
- Grayscale-to-Duotone-12
- Grayscale-to-Duotone-13
- Grayscale-to-Duotone-14
- Grayscale-to-Duotone-15
- Grayscale-to-Duotone-16
- Grayscale-to-Duotone-17
- Grayscale-to-Duotone-18
- Grayscale-to-Duotone-19
- Grayscale-to-Duotone-20
- Convert-to-Indexed-01
- Convert-to-Indexed-02
- Convert-to-Indexed-03
- Convert-to-Indexed-04
- Convert-to-Indexed-05
- Convert-to-Indexed-06
- Convert-to-Indexed-07
- Convert-to-Indexed-08
- Convert-to-Indexed-09
- Convert-to-Indexed-10
- RGB-to-Grayscale-to-Tritone01
- RGB-to-Grayscale-to-Tritone02
- RGB-to-Grayscale-to-Tritone03
- RGB-to-Grayscale-to-Tritone04
- RGB-to-Grayscale-to-Tritone05

- RGB-to-Grayscale-to-Tritone06
- RGB-to-Grayscale-to-Tritone07
- RGB-to-Grayscale-to-Tritone08
- RGB-to-Grayscale-to-Tritone09
- RGB-to-Grayscale-to-Tritone10
- RGB-to-Grayscale-to-Tritone11
- RGB-to-Grayscale-to-Tritone12
- RGB-to-Grayscale-to-Tritone13
- RGB-to-Grayscale-to-Tritone14
- RGB-to-Grayscale-to-Tritone15
- RGB-to-Grayscale-to-Tritone16
- RGB-to-Grayscale-to-Tritone17
- RGB-to-Grayscale-to-Tritone18
- RGB-to-Grayscale-to-Tritone19
- RGB-to-Grayscale-to-Tritone20
- RGB-to-Grayscale-to-Quadtone01
- RGB-to-Grayscale-to-Quadtone02
- RGB-to-Grayscale-to-Quadtone03
- RGB-to-Grayscale-to-Quadtone04
- RGB-to-Grayscale-to-Quadtone05
- RGB-to-Grayscale-to-Quadtone06
- RGB-to-Grayscale-to-Quadtone07
- RGB-to-Grayscale-to-Quadtone08
- RGB-to-Grayscale-to-Quadtone09
- RGB-to-Grayscale-to-Quadtone10
- RGB-to-Grayscale-to-Quadtone11
- RGB-to-Grayscale-to-Quadtone12
- RGB-to-Grayscale-to-Quadtone13
- RGB-to-Grayscale-to-Quadtone14
- RGB-to-Grayscale-to-Quadtone15
- RGB-to-Grayscale-to-Quadtone16
- RGB-to-Grayscale-to-Quadtone17
- RGB-to-Grayscale-to-Quadtone18
- RGB-to-Grayscale-to-Quadtone19

- RGB-to-Grayscale-to-Quadtone20
- RGB-to-CMYK
- RGB-to-Lab
- RGB-to-Multichannel
- RGB-AssignProfile-WorkingRGB
- AssignProfile-Adobe-RGB-1998
- AssignProfile-Apple_RGB
- AssignProfile-ColorMatch_RGB
- AssignProfile-CIE_RGB
- AssignProfile-DiamondTron_G22_D93
- AssignProfile-e-sRGB
- AssignProfile-GenericMonitor_2-2_Gamma
- AssignProfile-GenMon_1-8
- AssignProfile-HitachiMon_G22_D93
- AssignProfile-KODAK_DC
- AssignProfile-NEC_Multisync_Monitor
- AssignProfile-NTSC_1953
- AssignProfile-PAL_SECAM
- AssignProfile-ProPhoto_RGB
- AssignProfile-Ricoh_RussianSC_040402
- AssignProfile-ROMM-RGB
- AssignProfile-SMPTE-C
- AssignProfile-TrinMon_G22_D93
- AssignProfile-WideGamut_RGB
- RGB-Grayscale-Duotone01
- RGB-Grayscale-Duotone02
- RGB-Grayscale-Duotone03
- RGB-Grayscale-Duotone04
- RGB-Grayscale-Duotone05
- RGB-Grayscale-Duotone06
- RGB-Grayscale-Duotone07
- RGB-Grayscale-Duotone08
- RGB-Grayscale-Duotone09
- RGB-Grayscale-Duotone10

- RGB-Grayscale-Duotone11
- RGB-Grayscale-Duotone12
- RGB-Grayscale-Duotone13
- RGB-Grayscale-Duotone14
- RGB-Grayscale-Duotone15
- RGB-Grayscale-Duotone16
- RGB-Grayscale-Duotone17
- RGB-Grayscale-Duotone18
- RGB-Grayscale-Duotone19
- RGB-Grayscale-Duotone20
- RGB-Grayscale-Duotone21
- RGB-Grayscale-Duotone22
- RGB-Grayscale-Duotone23
- RGB-Grayscale-Duotone24
- RGB-Grayscale-Duotone25

Set: *PTK-AdjustmentLayers.atn*

Actions can help you create and manipulate adjustment layers in a snap. You can apply fill layers, curves, and even photo filters to the image or portions of the image without altering any pixels on the layers themselves.

- Color Fill Adjustment Layer
- Gradient Fill Adjustment Layer
- Pattern Fill Adjustment Layer
- Levels Adjustment Layer
- Curves Adjustment Layer
- Color Balance Adjustment Layer
- Brightness_Contrast Adjustment Layer
- Hue_Saturation Adjustment Layer
- Selective Color Adjustment Layer
- Channel Mixer Adjustment Layer
- Gradient Map Adjustment Layer
- Photo Filter-Warming 85
- Photo Filter-Warming 81
- Photo Filter-Cooling 80

- Photo Filter-Cooling 82
- Photo Filter-Red
- Photo Filter-Orange
- Photo Filter-Yellow
- Photo Filter-Green
- Photo Filter-Cyan
- Photo Filter-Blue
- Photo Filter-Violet
- Photo Filter-Magenta
- Photo Filter-Sepia
- Photo Filter-Deep Red
- Photo Filter-Deep Blue
- Photo Filter-Deep Emerald
- Photo Filter-Deep Yellow
- Photo Filter-Underwater
- Invert Adjustment Layer
- Threshold Adjustment Layer
- Posterize Adjustment Layer-2 levels
- Posterize Adjustment Layer-4 levels (example earlier in this guide)
- Posterize Adjustment Layer-6 levels
- Posterize Adjustment Layer-8 levels

Set: *Production_Set-01.atn*

This set of actions can help you decrease production time.

- Transform Selection
- Divide into Quarters
- Divide into Thirds
- Center Canvas
- Convert to Index
- Crop Selected Area
- Copy-Paste into New
- Copy-Paste-Index
- Make Layer
- Name Layer

- Duplicate-Index
- Create New Layer

Set: *Production_Set-02.atn*

This set of actions also helps you decrease production time.

- Duplicate Document
- Duplicate_Background-New_Document
- Step_Backward
- Step_Forward
- Define_Image_As_Pattern
- Purge_Histories
- Purge_Undo
- Purge_All
- ActionsPalette-Button Mode
- Close
- Curves
- Duplicate Layer
- Fade
- Flatten
- Gaussian Blur
- Image Size
- Lab Mode
- Levels
- New
- Open
- Print
- RGB Mode
- Save As
- Unsharp Mask
- Make Gradient
- Color Balance
- CanvasSize-125x125
- Calculations
- Reveal_All
- Trim

Set: *PTK-Additional Layer Actions.atn*

This set contains dozens of actions that you can use to manipulate layers and layer properties.

- New Fill Layer-Solid Color
- New Fill Layer-Gradient
- New Fill Layer-Pattern
- New Layer From Background
- New Layer Set
- Duplicate Layer Set
- Layer Set Properties
- Rasterize Current Layer
- Rasterize All Layers
- Rasterize Type-Current Layer
- New Layer Based Slice
- Add Layer Mask-Reveal All
- Add Layer Mask-Hide All
- Disable Layer Mask
- Enable Layer Mask
- Add Vector Mask-Reveal All
- Delete Vector Mask
- Add Vector Mask-Hide All
- Disable Vector Mask
- Create Clipping Mask
- Release Clipping Mask
- Arrange-Send Backward
- Arrange-Bring Forward
- Arrange-Send to Back
- Arrange-Bring to Front
- Align Linked-Top Edges
- Align Linked-Vertical Centers
- Align Linked-Bottom Edges
- Align Linked-Left Edges
- Align Linked-Horizontal Centers
- Align Linked-Right Edges

- Distribute Linked-Top Edges
- Distribute Linked-Vertical Centers
- Distribute Linked-Bottom Edges
- Distribute Linked-Left Edges
- Distribute Linked-Horizontal Centers
- Distribute Linked-Right Edges
- Lock Linked Layers-Transparency
- Lock Linked Layers-Position
- Lock Linked Layers-Trans_Pos
- Lock Linked Layers-Image
- Lock Linked Layers-Image_Pos
- Lock Linked Layers-All
- Merge Linked
- Merge Visible
- Flatten Image
- Matting-Defringe
- Matting-Remove Black Matte
- Matting-Remove White Matte
- Layer-Merge Down
- New-Layer via Copy
- New-Layer via Cut

Set: PTK-Align_Layer_Group.atn

These actions give you control over the orientation of your layers on the document, whether to the left, right, top, center, and so on.

- Horizontal Center
- Vertical Center
- Exact Center (example earlier in this guide)
- Top Edge
- Bottom Edge
- Left Edge
- Right Edge
- Left Center
- Bottom Left

- Bottom Center
- Bottom Right
- Top Left
- Top Center
- Top Right

Set: *PTK-Path Tools.atn*

You can use actions to manipulate and transform paths. You can save, duplicate, create selections from, and rotate paths with a mouse click.

- Save Path
- Duplicate Path
- Delete Path
- Clipping Path
- Make Selection of Path
- Transform Path-Scale (example earlier in this guide)
- Rotate Path 180 degrees
- Rotate Path 90 degrees CW
- Rotate Path 90 degrees CCW
- Flip Path Horizontal
- Flip Path Vertical

Set: *PTK-Selections.atn*

Manipulating selections just became easier with actions that put control over them a mouse click away.

- Select All
- Deselect
- Select Inverse
- Select Color Range
- Feather Selection
- Modify Border
- Modify-Smooth
- Modify-Expand
- Modify-Contract
- Select-Grow

- Select Similar
- Transform Selection
- Save Selection

Set: *RGB-Channel-Actions.atn*

You can duplicate your channels either within the same document or by creating new documents altogether.

- Red_Duplicate-Same_Document
- Green_Duplicate-Same_Document
- Blue_Duplicate-Same_Document
- Red_Duplicate-New_Document
- Green_Duplicate-New_Document
- Blue_Duplicate-New_Document

Set: *Snapshots.atn*

A quick way to ensure you do not lose your histories is to take a quick snapshot when you reach a stopping point.

- Snapshot-Full_Doc
- Snapshot-Merged_Layers
- Snapshot-Current_Layer

Set: *TransparencyGrids.atn*

Tired of those little gray squares? Wish they were bigger? Whatever your taste, you can manipulate them with these actions.

- TransparencyGrid-Off
- TransparencyGrid-SmallGray
- TransparencyGrid-MediumGray
- TransparencyGrid-LargeGray

Typography

You can build and use actions for many purposes beyond photography. Because text and type are probably the next most common image element, I've given you a great start into using actions in this area. The actions in this section of the CD all work with the Type and Type Mask tools, helping you create and modify text.

Type actions can cover a gamut of results, and this section reflects that. You can use actions to automate the characteristics of text—paragraphs, justification, and normal adjustments you might expect in word-processing software. But Photoshop can go much farther than that.

In Photoshop, you can also generate image effects in the shape of type. For instance, you can create text that appears to be made of molten metal, wood, layered plastic, and so forth. You can save these techniques as actions and then use them time and again as needed. This section attempts to cover both aspects of type. Some actions handle standard type tool adjustments that you can use in a word processor. I've also included dozens of special effects–style type.

Sample Typography Actions

AFX-CloudsOverWaterCS

You can produce dramatic effects over type elements with a wide variety of text-based actions. AFX-CloudsOverWaterCS creates a random blue/white sky look inside any text you enter. To try this, load the action set (in the Typography section of the CD) and proceed with the following steps. (This action will create its own document, so don't worry about having a file open.)

1. Expand the CloudsOverWaterCS action set.
2. Select the action CloudsOverWaterCS.
3. Click the Play Selection button at the bottom of the Actions palette.
4. Follow the directions that appear carefully. In this particular action, the only command that you need really be concerned about is entering the text with the Type Mask tool, instead of the standard Type tool. The Type Mask tool appears as a capitol *T* made of dotted lines, or "marching ants". When this command appears, be sure to use a large font size as requested in the Stop message.
5. After you meet the conditions in the Stop message, click the Play Selection button again.
6. After the action plays through to the final Stop message, click OK.

Your new document should have created text that appears to be filled with cloudy variations between white and blue, with a rough outline around the text.

AFX-OiledMetalCS-1

This action is also in the Typography section of the Toolkit CD. Note the Continue and Stop buttons. The person recording an action can cause a hard stop or let the user continue without taking any action. Since this message is simply for information, no action is required. Click Continue to proceed with the playback.

During the course of the action, you may be requested to change a setting or insert text. If you follow the directions carefully as given by the action and continue running through to completion, you should receive results similar if not identical to those achieved when the action was recorded.

AFX-RumpledSatin and AFX-WildStripes

You can add steps to an action anywhere by simply recording them at the appropriate time. For example, load AFX-RumpledSatin.atn from the CD, and play the action through to completion, being careful to follow the Stop messages. You can see the end result of this action as recorded in the first image.

You can easily add commands to exisiting actions at any point within the action.

1. Select the last command performed just prior to the final Stop message, and click the Record button.

2. Record additional commands by simply manipulating the current image.

3. Stop recording.

4. I recommend you save the new recording as a new action and/or an action set.

In the second image, you can see the results of the new action created by adding steps. The layered PSD file for this image is available in the Chapter 2 folder on the CD.

Warp Text-Rise-Horiz

This action (in the PTK-Type Tools.atn action set) applies the warp called Rise to your text. It is fully customizable. Other actions in this set allow you to apply other warp settings directly to your text.

All Typography Actions

Some actions in the Typography section are standalone files or in an action set by the same name:

- DigiCheckersCS
- TextureTypeCS
- AFX-CloudsOverWaterCS (example earlier in this guide)
- AFX-OiledMetalCS-1 (example earlier in this guide)
- AFX-RumpledSatin (example earlier in this guide)
- AFX-WildStripes (example earlier in this guide)

Set: _PTK-TYPE-CS-Set01.atn_

- AFX-AlphaNoiseCS
- AFX-BloodyAlienCS
- AlienNeonCS
- ArizonaCS
- ArtisanCS
- ArtisanCS-ver2
- ArtisanCS-ver3
- ArtisanCS-ver4
- ArtisanCS-ver5
- ArtisanCS-ver6
- WesternLeatherCS
- ScreendoorSunsetCS
- CabinetCS
- Gold-In-PlasticCS
- ButterMeltCS
- ThePitsCS
- StacksCS
- RiverStoneCS
- AFX-WaterPlantsCS

Set: _PTK-MetallicTypeCS.atn_

- AFX-MetalStainCS-01
- AFX-MetalStainCS-02
- AFX-CopperCS-01
- AFX-CopperPlatedCS-01
- AFX-MetalVialCS
- AFX-RoyalGoldCS
- AFX-CHROMECS-01
- AFX-AnimetalCS-01
- AFX-BoldMetalCS-01
- AFX-HarshTarnishCS
- AFX-HarshTarnishCS-02
- AFX-BronzeVariantCS-01

- AFX-BronzeVariantCS-02
- AFX-WackyChromeCS-01
- AFX-FoiledCS-01
- AFX-MetalMasterCS-01
- AFX-LiquidMetalCS-01
- AFX-GoldOreCS-01

Set: *PTK-Type Tools.atn*

Not to be confused with Typography actions (in a different section on the CD), these actions help you modify your fonts, whether through aliasing or warping. Convert type to a shape, change between Paragraph Text and Point Text, and align text on your image.

- Create Work Path
- Convert to Shape
- Horizontal to Vertical
- Vertical to Horizontal
- Anti-Alias None
- Anti-Alias-Sharp
- Anti-Alias-Crisp
- Anti-Alias Strong
- Anti-Alias Smooth
- Convert to Paragraph Text
- Convert to Point Text
- Warp Text-Arc-Horiz
- Warp Text-Arc Lower-Horiz
- Warp Text-Arc Upper-Horiz
- Warp Text-Arch-Horiz
- Warp Text-Bulge-Horiz
- Warp Text-Shell Lower-Horiz
- Warp Text-Shell Upper-Horiz
- Warp Text-Flag-Horiz
- Warp Text-Wave-Horiz
- Warp Text-Fish-Horiz
- Warp Text-Rise-Horiz (example earlier in this guide)

- Warp Text-Fisheye-Horiz

- Warp Text-Inflate-Horiz

- Warp Text-Squeeze-Horiz

- Warp Text-Twist-Horiz

- Left Align Text

- Center Text

- Right Align Text

Additional Plug-Ins and Add-Ons

This section includes additional goodies, which I built, that you can plug right into
Photoshop and use to explore your artistic talents: brushes, patterns, custom shapes,
and layer styles.

Brushes

Each of these brush sets contains multiple brushes, giving you well over 100 additional goodies to plug in to Photoshop. You can load each set using the Brushes Preset
Picker menu.

- `afx-books001.abr`

- `afx-books002.abr`

- `afx-books003.abr`

- `afx-books004.abr`

- `afx-chemical001.abr`

- `afx-civilEng001.abr`

- `afx-dance001.abr`

- `afx-dance002.abr`

- `afx-electrical1001.abr`

- `afx-electrical002.abr`

- `afx-electrical003.abr`

- `afx-electrical004.abr`

- `afx-energy001.abr`

- `afx-energy002.abr`

- `afx-energy003.abr`

- `afx-energy004.abr`

- `afx-fantasy001.abr`

- afx-fantasy002.abr
- afx-fantasy003.abr
- afx-fantasy004.abr
- afx-rulers001.abr
- afx-school001.abr
- afx-school002.abr
- afx-school003.abr
- afx-writing001.abr
- afx-writing002.abr
- afx-writing003.abr
- afx-writing004.abr

Custom Pattern Sets

You can use patterns as backgrounds and apply them to layer styles as patterns and textures. Each set contains multiple patterns.

- 031703001.pat
- 031703002.pat
- 031703003.pat
- 031703004.pat
- 031703005.pat
- 031703006.pat
- 031703007.pat
- 031703008.pat
- 031703009.pat
- 031703010.pat
- 031703011.pat
- 031703012.pat

Custom Shapes

You can use the following custom vector shapes in your designs. Each set has multiple shapes.

- AFX-Arrows1.csh
- AFX-Arrows2.csh
- AFX-Arrows3.csh
- AFX-Arrows4.csh

- AFX-CropCircleSet001.csh
- AFX-CropCircleSet002.csh
- AFX-CropCircleSet003.csh
- AFX-CropCircleSet004.csh
- AFX-CropCircleSet005.csh
- AFX-Dings001.csh
- AFX-Oddities1.csh

Layer Styles

The layer styles in these sets are designed to work on type and frames. Each set contains 10 or more styles, adding more than 200 additional effects for your text or images.

- single-blank.asl: This set contains a single style that will reset/remove all applied styles on a layer.
- PTK-TypeStyles01.asl
- PTK-TypeStyles02.asl
- PTK-TypeStyles03.asl
- PTK-TypeStyles04.asl
- PTK-TypeStyles05.asl
- PTK-TypeStyles06.asl
- PTK-TypeStyles07.asl
- PTK-TypeStyles08.asl
- PTK-TypeStyles09.asl
- PTK-TypeStyles10.asl
- PTK-TypeStyles11.asl
- PTK-TypeStyles12.asl
- PTK-TypeStyles13.asl
- PTK-TypeStyles14.asl
- PTK-TypeStyles15.asl
- PTK-TypeStyles16.asl
- PTK-TypeStyles17.asl
- PTK-TypeStyles18.asl
- PTK-TypeStyles19.asl
- PTK-TypeStyles20.asl
- PTK-TypeStyles21.asl
- PTK-TypeStyles22.asl

Third-Party Actions, Add-Ons, and Stock Images

I've been speaking about the power of actions for years, and when I started, few people, online or elsewhere, took them seriously. Thankfully that has changed, as more people every day realize the potential of Photoshop's automating capabilities.

This portion of the CD contains the work of some fine contributors who have also taken up the torch, dedicating their time and knowledge to furthering the cause of automation. It is my pleasure to include a sampling of their work in this book, and I'm certain you will find their contributions interesting and helpful.

Action_Dex-Windows

ActionDex is a new piece of software by Keith Davidson that helps action users and creators manage their libraries of scripts. Although only available for Windows at the time of this writing, ActionDex takes care of some of the more frustrating aspects of managing actions. Here's what ActionDex has to say about itself:

> *ActionDex by PicsToBits solves a frequent problem for Photoshop users—organizing and managing hundreds or thousands of actions so they are easy to find. After defining a hierarchy of categories (much like folders in Windows Explorer), you can organize your actions and action sets into logical task-based groupings to reflect your personal work style. Actions can even be placed in multiple categories and you can add notes to keep track of favorite settings, tips, etc. Of course a picture is worth a thousand words so ActionDex can automatically create a preview image and associate it with an action for easy visual reference of the effect an action produces. ActionDex also allows you to create backup copies of your entire actions palette.*

Trust me: the preview image feature alone is worth its weight in gold to action guys like me! You can visit the creator's website at `http://picstobits.com`.

Robert Anselmi

Robert is *the man* behind ChainStyle.com and has his own series of excellent Photoshop add-ons that have been making a splash in the online community. We have a mutual interest in promoting and creating actions, and as a result of that interest and our conversations, Robert has become a good friend. An excellent action creator, he is also a teacher and has supplied not only actions but PDF tutorials that you may find useful.

You will find the following in this folder.

Set: *Assorted Photo Frames.atn*

- Colored Glass with Flare (170px)
- Stacked Glass over Neblula (75px)

- Clear Glass (50px)
- Matted Pink/Grey (250px)
- Green & Gold Flare Matte (210px)
- Scratched & Striped (200px)
- Marble Stone Matte (150px)
- Brushed Copper Matte Frame (150 px)
- Copper Jungle Matte (225px)
- Brushed Copper (70 px)
- Titanium Steel (50px)
- Authentic Chrome (150px)
- Layered Metals on Canvas (100px)
- Ball-Bearing Cylinder (200px)
- Reflective Metallic Illusions (200px)
- Oval Aluminum Edge
- Oval Rainbow Freakout Frame (300px)
- Metallic Pond Drop (150px)
- Candy Wrapper Red/Blue (60px)
- Impossible Frame 1 (150px)
- Cheetah - Large Spots (75px)
- Giraffe Frame (150px)
- Spiral Stroke Frame 2 (100px)
- Red Nightmare (100px)
- Various B/W Line Art Patterns (175px)
- Crushed Velvet Frame (135px)
- Blood Orange (100px)
- Rainbow Gone Haywire (150px)
- H Perspective Left (400×300)
- H Image Distort Top-Right (400×300)

Set: *Backdrops & Canvases.atn*

- Carnival Backdrop
- Fishtank Floor
- Hellraiser Backdrop
- Painted Backdrop

- Egyptian Wall
- Dual Plaid
- 3D Plumbing Pipes
- Colored Glass Mosaic
- Foil
- Melting Mercury
- Candy Canvas
- Sandy Shore
- Earth from Above
- Metal Rivets (Medium)
- Thatched Backdrop
- Spiderman Web
- Wood Panelling (Vertical)

Set: *Design Color Tools.atn*

- Find All Color Combinations
- Find a Complimentary Color
- Find a Color Triad
- Find Analogous Colors
- Find Split Complementary Colors
- Find Monochromatic Colors
- Create Swatches from Image

Set: *Digital Cross Processing.atn*

- Digital Cross Process 1
- Digital Cross Process 2
- Digital Cross Process 3
- Digital Cross Process 4
- Digital Cross Process 5
- Digital Cross Process 6
- Digital Cross Process 7
- Digital Cross Process 8
- Digital Cross Process 9
- Digital Cross Process 10
- Digital Cross Process 11

Set: *Edges & Corner Frames.atn*

- Dry Brush Corners
- Dry Brush Corners Alternate
- Cutout Corners
- Pencil Stroke Corners
- Film Grain Edges
- Film Grain Edges Alternate
- Fresco Corners
- Glow Corners
- Palette Knife Corners
- Plastic Wrap Corners
- Plastic Wrap Corners Alternate
- Poster Edges Corners
- Rough Pastel Corners 1
- Rough Pastel Corners 2
- Rough Pastel Corners 3
- Rough Pastel Corners 4
- Smudge Stick Corners 1
- Smudge Stick Corners 2
- Smudge Stick Corners 3
- Sponge Corners 1
- Sponge Corners 2
- Watercolor Corners 1
- Watercolor Corners 2
- Watercolor Corners 3
- Accented Edges 1
- Angled Stroke Corners 1
- Angled Stroke Corners 2
- Crosshatch Corners 1
- Crosshatch Corners 2
- Crosshatch Corners 3

Set: *Photo Actions.atn*

- Blown Out
- Sepia Tone Generator (Light)

- Sepia Tone Generator (Mid)
- Sepia Tone Generator (Dark)
- Cross-Process 1
- Cross-Process 2
- Cross-Process 3
- Cross Process 4
- Jazz Style
- Art Deco Style
- Cartoon Style
- Silkscreen
- Plastic Doll (Mild)
- Plastic Doll (Strong)
- BW Underex Tint
- Dream Painter 1
- Dream Painter 2
- Underex Correct 1
- ColorCast Correct
- ST Aged Photo 2

Set: *More Photo Actions.atn*

- Thick Line Painting (Color)
- Thick Line Painting (Color 2)
- Thick Line Painting (Color 3)
- Thick Line Painting (Color Inverted)
- Thick Line Painting (Color Inverted 2)
- Thick Line Painting (B&W)
- Thick Line Painting (B&W Inverted)
- Chrome Painting (Color)
- Chrome Painting (B&W)
- Plastic Painting (Color)
- Medium Cartoon (Color)
- Light Cartoon (Color)
- Dark Cartoon (Color)

- Light Cartoon (Toned-down)
- Dark Cartoon (Toned-down)

Set: *Pattern Generators.atn*

- PATTERN SET GENERATOR 5
- JPG-WEB-DMAP GENERATOR 5 (PS7)
- Dark Visions
- Stark Visions
- Ice Flakes
- Cathedral
- Wind Dance
- Quills
- Concavity
- Rings
- Chopped
- Walkways
- Flume
- Eternity
- Feathers
- Parlor
- Rotor
- Rhythm
- Polar Fun
- Skydiving
- Whacked
- Wave Shuttle
- Corners
- Lost Compass
- Motion
- Glamor
- Vertigo

Set: *Red Eye and Watermark.atn*

- Red Eye Correction
- Watermark Your Image

Set: *ReTexture Generators.atn*

- TEXTURE SET GENERATOR 1
- JPG-WEB-DMAP GENERATOR 1 (PS7)
- Metallic Rock
- Plastic Rock
- Light Waves
- Forest
- Satin Cushion
- Stoneface
- Gothic
- Vascular
- Dry Brush
- Molten
- Motion Map
- Glue Gun
- Smoke
- Mottled
- Gooey
- Scaley
- Electricity
- Geometric
- Parabolic Square
- Gems
- Cyclone
- Wallpaper Peel
- Rubylith Star
- Falling Star
- Mountain Map

Set: *Wood Frames.atn*

- Burled Myrtle (100px)
- Cracked Wood Frame (200px)
- Pomele Sapele (125px)
- Ivory Needlewood (125px)

- English Brown Oak (100px)
- Masur Birch (160px)
- African Padouk (130px)
- Jelutong (130px)
- Cocobolo (75px)
- Madrone (125px)
- Bocote Light (150px)
- Amboyna (100px)
- Camphor Burl (75px)
- Burled Afzelia (75px)

Tutorials (PDF Format)

- Branching your Actions.pdf
- ChainStyle Action Samples.pdf
- Correcting Underexposure.pdf
- Creating a Color Scheme.pdf
- Working with Masks for Edge and Frame Effects.pdf

Danny Raphael

Danny moderates the Photo-art Forum at http://retouchpRO.com and is an excellent action creator. Enjoy his artistry and expertise!

Set: *djr 7ART-Checkerboard Selection.atn*

- Readme
- Djr 7ART-Checkerboard Selection

Set: *djr ART.atn*

- djr ART 10x10 Grid by Stroke
- djr ART Channel Swap 1 Mixer
- djr ART Chrome Sketch LindaV
- djr ART Lisa Neal Offset v3.0
- djr ART Oils by Ted LaCascio v2
- djr ART Oils via CNC
- djr ART Paint Slap
- djr ART Solarize on Steroids

- djr ART7 LeRoy Like
- dr-ART Watercolor #24 copy
- djr ART7 Wind-n-Edge

Set: *djr ART-Panes a Plenty.atn*

- djr Panes 1 Setup - run me first
- djr Panes 2 Create Panes copy
- djr Panes 3 Finish up

Set: *djr ART-Virtual Painter.atn*

- Readme
- djr Virtual Painter 3 variations v3r1
- djr Virtual Painter 4 variations v1r0

Set: *djr BW, Edges, Frames, Utility.atn*

- djr BW-Ansel Adams Effect
- djr BW Grayscale Options and Snaps v3r1
- djr BW Grayscale Options v3
- djr BW Russell Brown method v3
- djr EDGE Halftone Dots v1
- djr EDGE Halftone Dots v2
- djr UTL 3x3 Guides
- djr UTL 50% Gray
- djr UTL Drop out color
- djr UTL SavingLayersToSeparateFiles

Kent Christiansen

Kent has graciously contributed an action set (Kent's BW selective color2.21.atn) containing three excellent color-mod actions:

- Hue/Sat + Selective Color
- RGB Channel Mix + Selective Color
- CMYK Chan Mix + Selective Color

Mike Finn

Mike Finn sent in several sets of actions that can give your photos the looks of fine paintings. Give them a try.

Mike Finns Amateur Painter.atn

- Readme
- Simplify
- Horizontal Image START
- Vertical Image START
- Amateur Painter
- Paper Texture
- Canvas Texture
- About

Mike Finns Antique_Book.atn

- Readme
- Antique Book

Mike Finns Insta-Paint.atn

- Insta-Paint

Mike Finns Insta-Sketch_Beta.atn

- Insta-sketch_Beta

Mike Finns Mike_Finns_Darkroom.atn

- LAB Sharpen
- Clarifier
- Colour Enhance
- Lift Shadows
- Grayscale
- 50% Gray Layer

Mike Finns Paint Tools_4.atn

- Simplify
- Oil Painting
- Water/Oils
- Digi Painting (Layers)
- Stress 3D (Layer)
- Stress (Layer)

- Art Class (Layer)
- Displace
- Texture (Layer)
- Edge Effect (Layer)
- Sprayed Strokes (Layer)

Mike Finns Pixel_Painter.atn

- Readme
- Pixel Painter

Mike Finns pOpArTiSt.atn

- pOpArTiSt
- Adjust pOpArTiSt

Mike Finns Watercolor.atn

- Watercolor

Stock and Practice Images

This section includes the images mentioned in the text of Chapters 2 and 3 and used in the walk-through portions of the book. The stock images are used by permission of PhotoSpin.com.

Stock Images	PSD Practice Files
0010039_HIGH.JPG	cloudyText.psd
0770143_HIGH.jpg	metalText.psd
1150002_HIGH.jpg	wildStripes.psd
lookingDown.jpg	Sharpening-2.psd
rustyMetal.jpg	
sweetGirl.jpg	

Index

A

Accelerated (playback) option, *12*, **12**, 41

Action Fx Photoshop Resources site, 79–80, 82

Action Options command/dialog box, 9, *12*, **12**, *42*, **42**

action sets, *See also* CD contents

  versus actions, 25, 27, *27*

  creating, 10, *10*

  loading into Actions palette menu

    from CDs/external drives, 23

    loading too many, 22–23, *23*

    from other folders, 22, *23*

    steps in, 22, 24

  renaming, 54

  saved in Presets subfolder, 13–14, *14*, 22, *22*

  saving as text files, 3–4, 76–79, *77–78*

  viewing in List mode, 7, 15, *15*

actions, *See also* CD contents; recording; Stop

  versus action sets, 25, 27, *27*

  color-coding

    using Action Options dialog box, 12, *12*

    using New Action dialog box, 10, *10*

    tips on, 76

    viewing in Button mode, 59, *59*

  compatibility issues

    between products, 74

    operating systems, 75

    overview, 74

    Photoshop versions, 74–75

  defined, **2**

  editing

    Action Options, 42, *42*

    adding commands from other actions, 40–41, *40*

    adding steps, 36–38, *37–38*

    deleting steps, 38–39, *39*

    duplicating commands, 39, *39*

    overview, 29–30

    Playback Options, *35*, 41–42

    rearranging actions, 17

    rearranging commands, 36, *36*

    rerecording commands, 34–36, *35*

    toggling command dialogs on/off, 31–34, *32–34*

    toggling commands on/off, 30–31, *31*

  online resources for, 79–80

  opening camera raw files with, 79

  overview, 1–2, 21, 71

  playing, *See also* Batch

    in batches, 61–66, *62–66*

    in Button mode, 25–27, *25–26*

    via Droplets, 19, 20, 66–67, *67–68*

    in List mode, 27–29, *27–29*

    multiple, at once, 16–17, *17*

    overview, 25

    skipped commands problem, 74

    Stop messages in, 26, *26*, 28–29, *28–29*

  saving, 13, 24–25, *25*, 53–54, *53–54*

  tips

    color-coding, 76

    keyboard shortcuts, 76

    naming, 76

    saving, 76–79, *77–78*

    Stop messages, 75

Type Mask tool, 28, *28*, 70
Typography actions. *See* CD contents

V

viewing
    in Button mode
        color-coding, 59, *59*
        default actions, 7–8, *8*
    in List mode
        action sets, 7, 15, *15*
        actions, 7, 15, *15*
        command settings, 16, *16*
        commands, 7, 9, 15, *16*

W

website addresses
    Action Fx (author's), 79, 82
    actions resources, 79–80
    Fred Miranda, 80
    HiddenElements, 74
    HTML Center, 80
    Keith Davidson, 124
    NAPP, 80
    Photo-art Forum, 131
    Photoshop Café, 80
    Photoshop User, 80
wildStripes.psd, 38

Photoshop® CS Titles

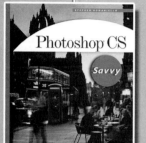
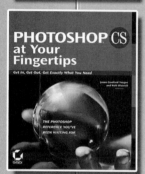
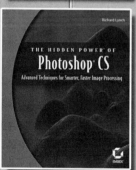
 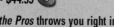

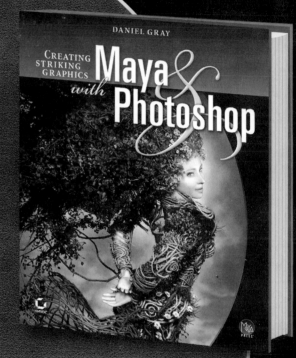